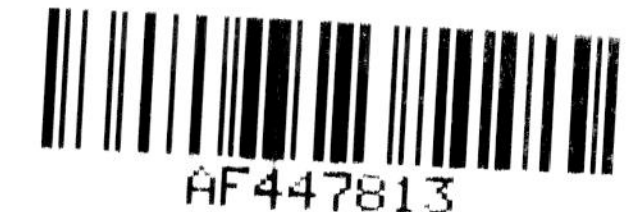

THIS COLORING BOOK
BELONGS TO :

____

- -

____

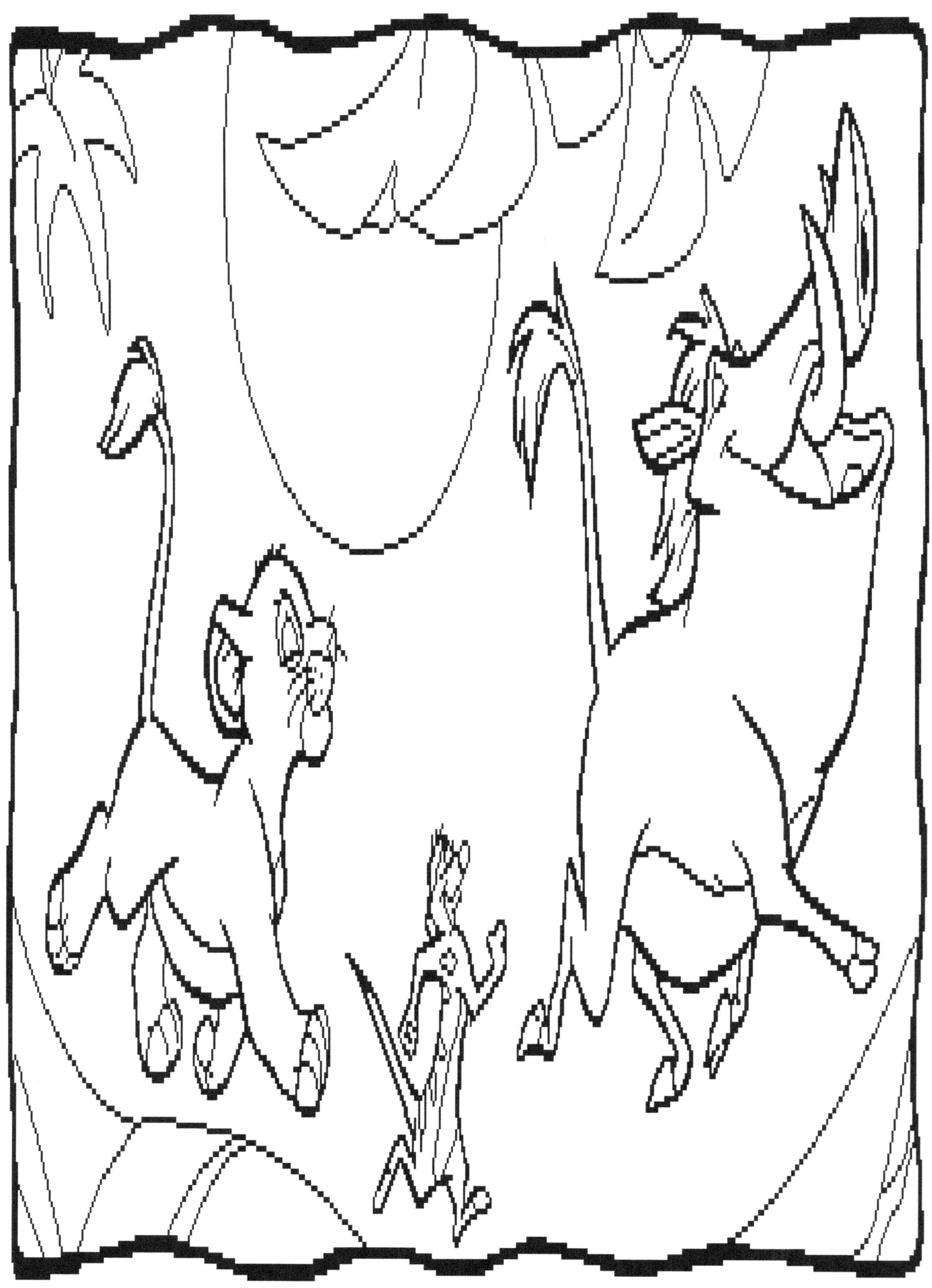

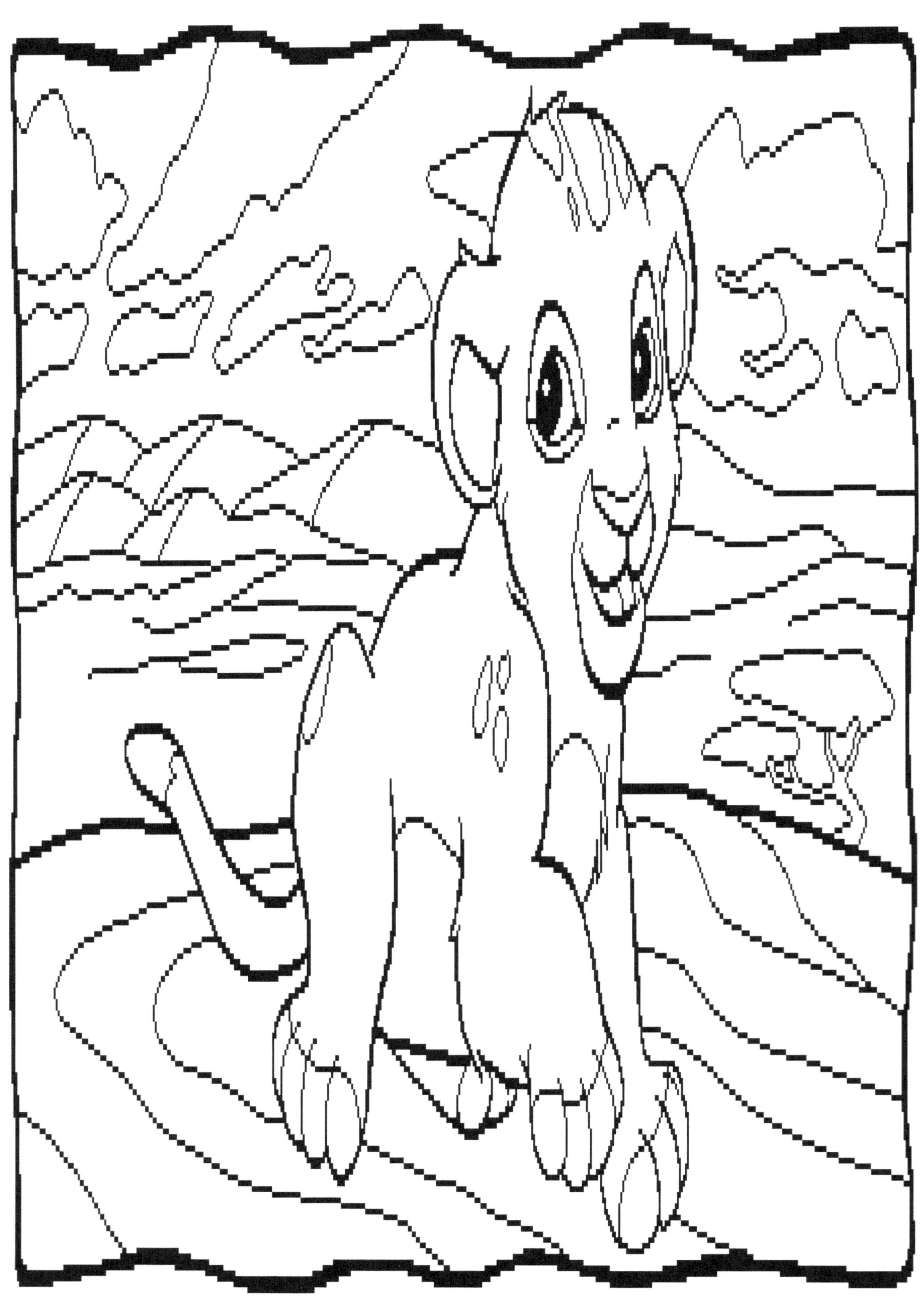

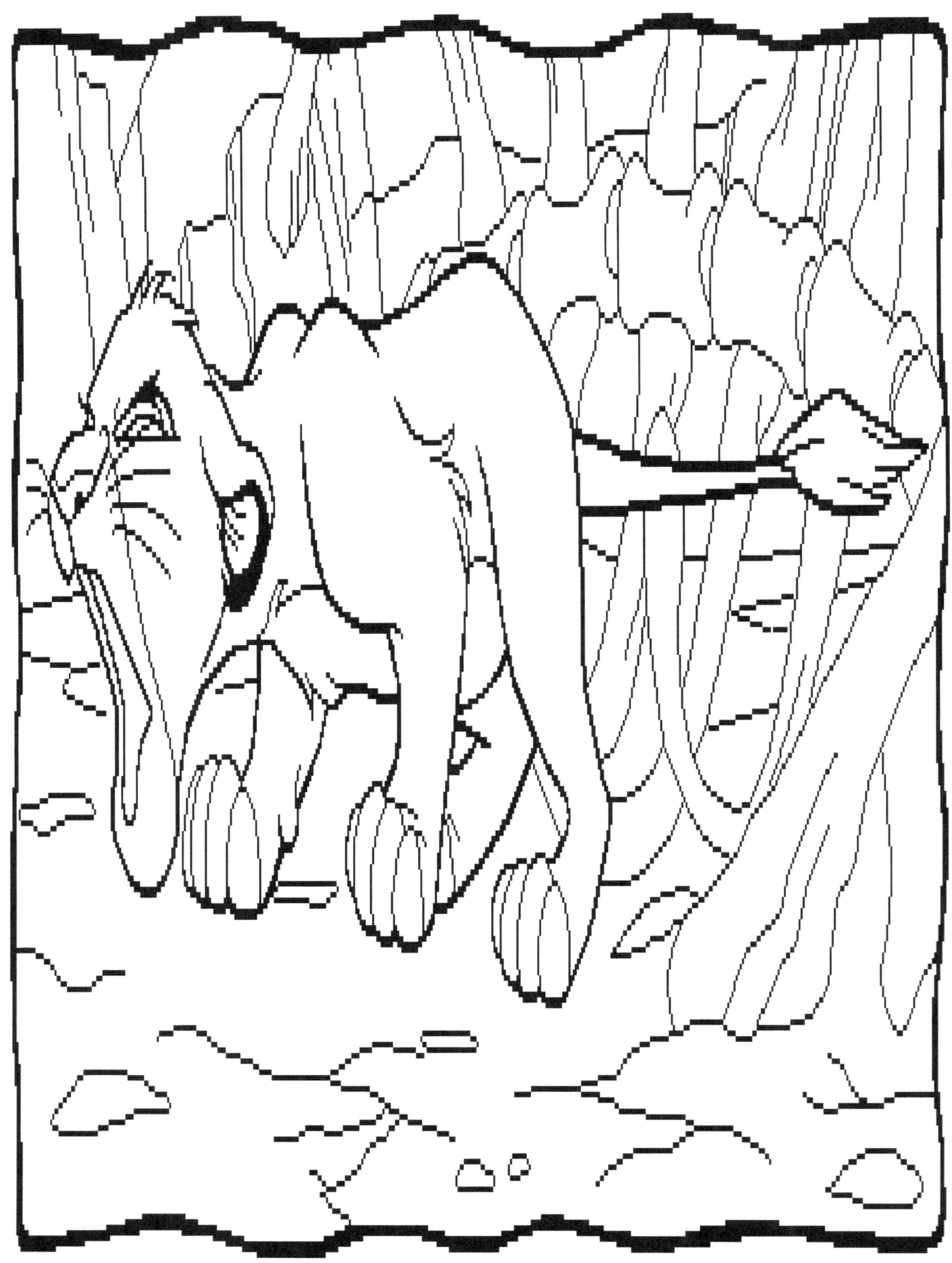

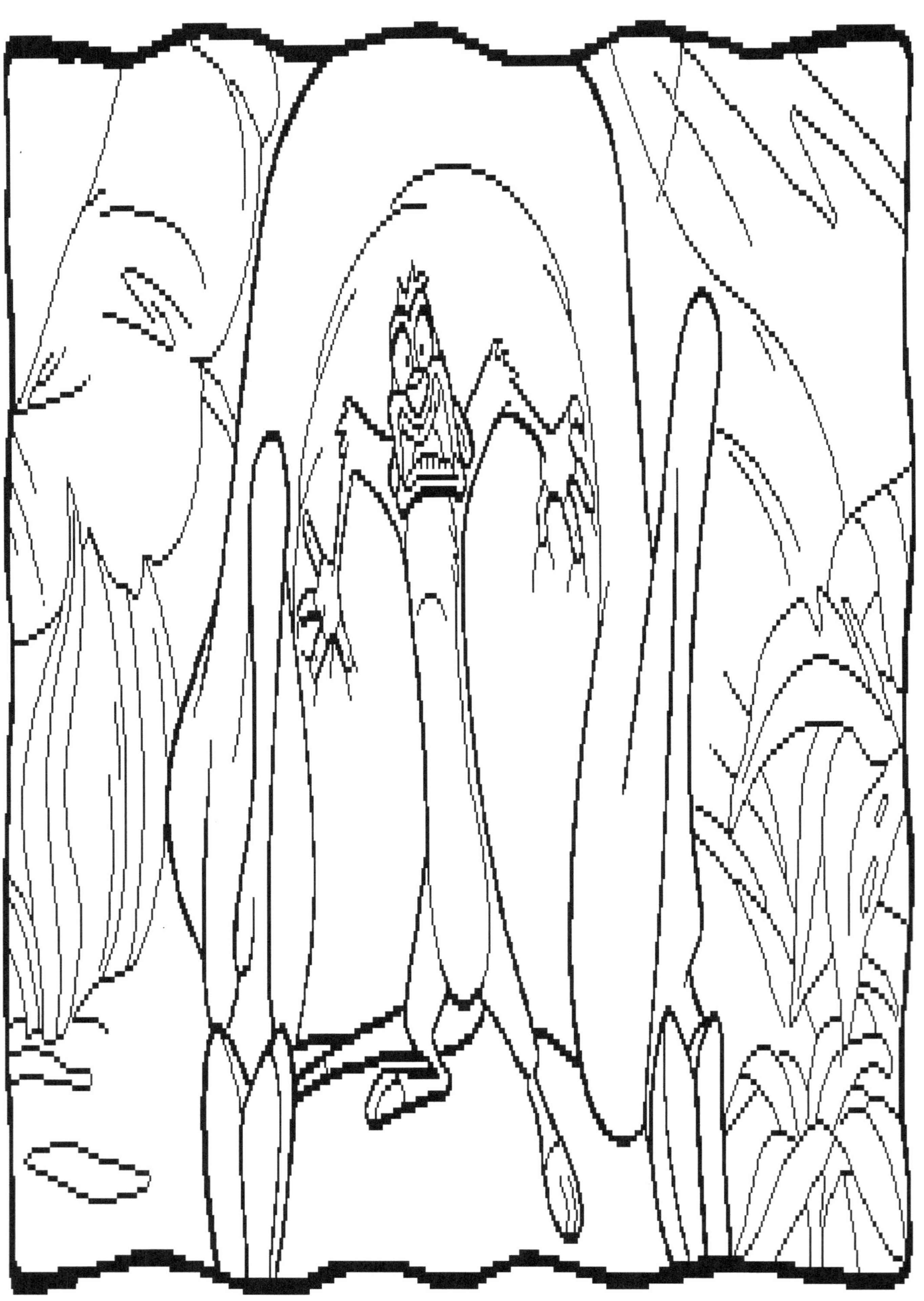

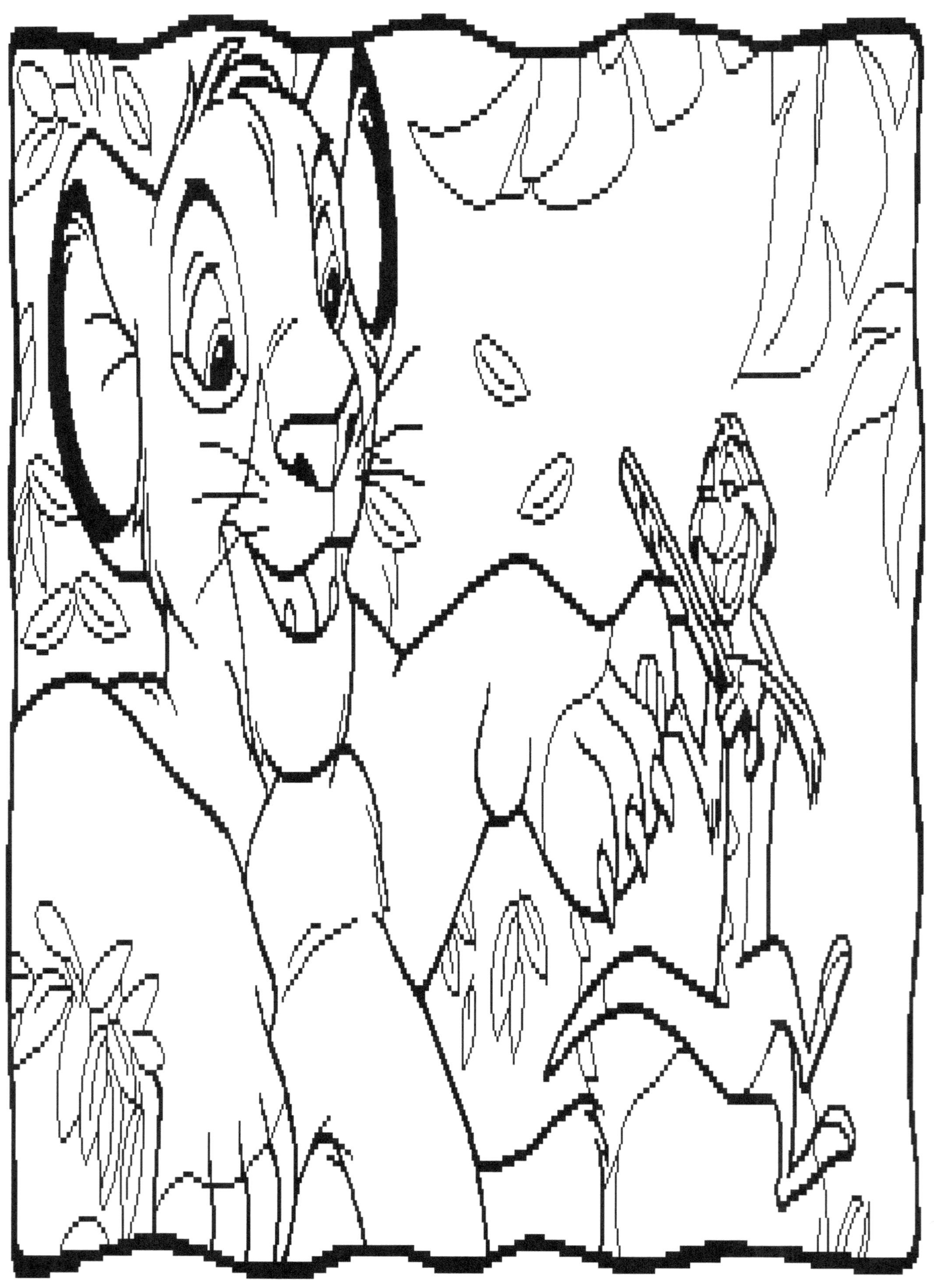

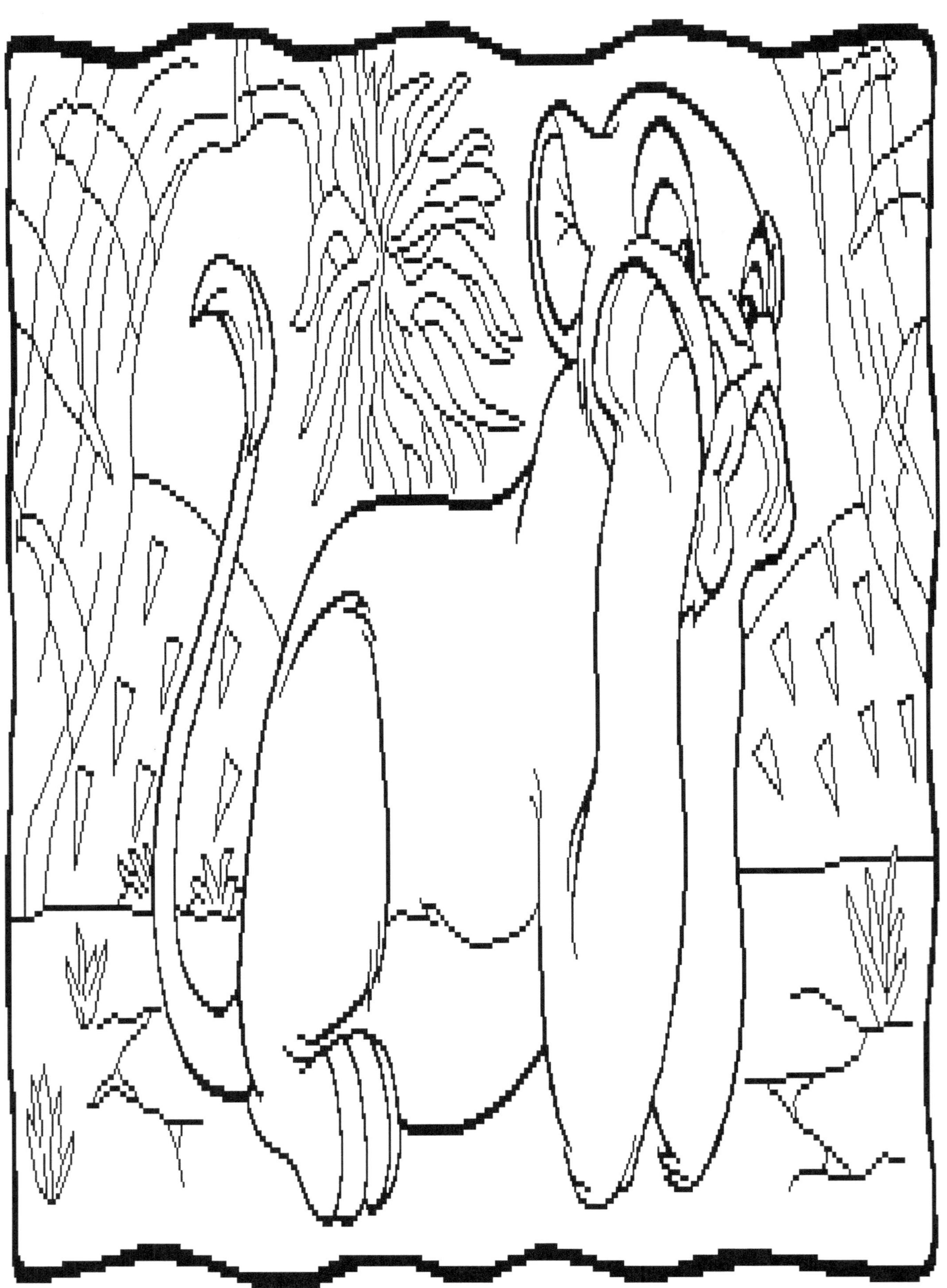

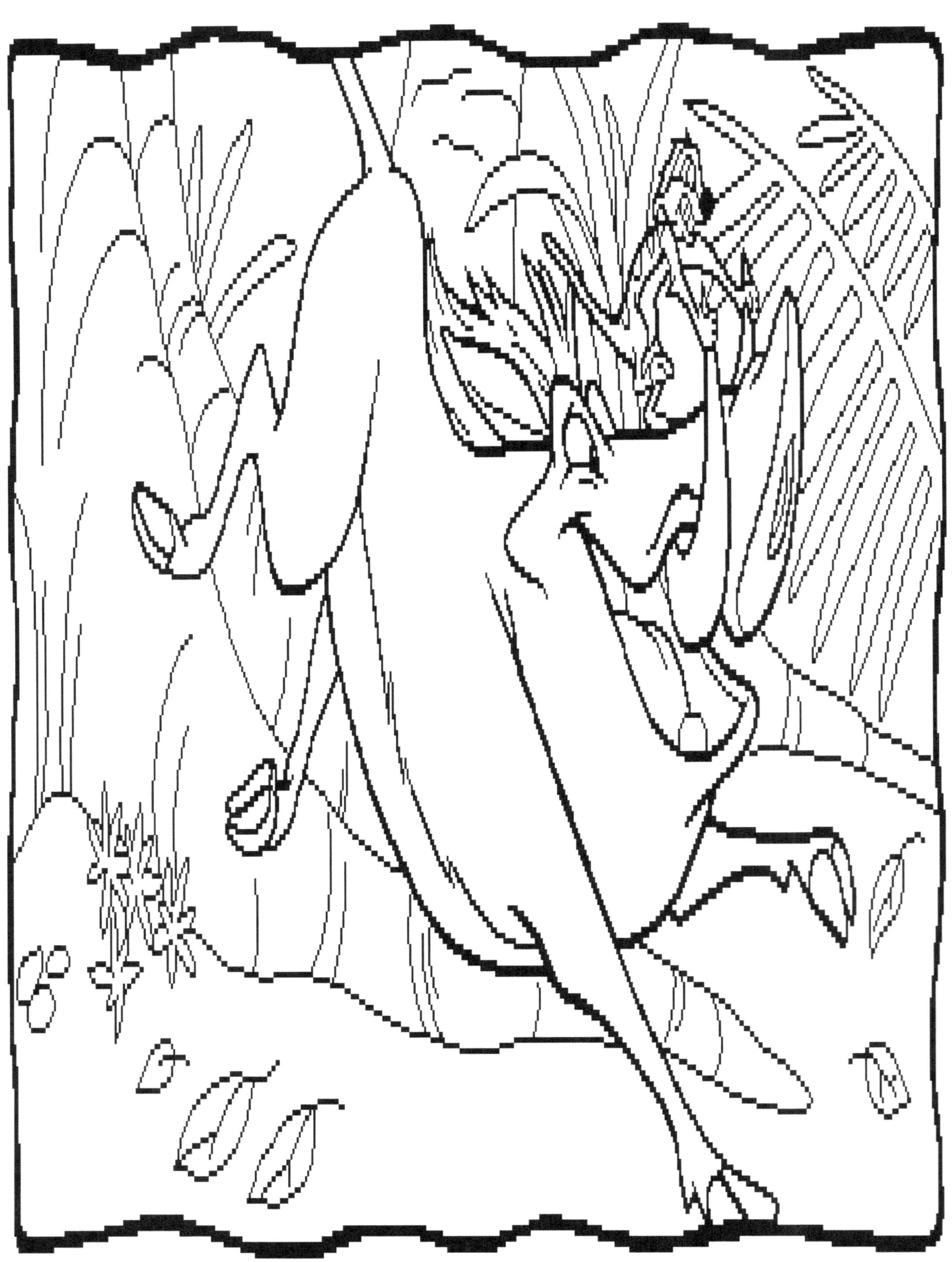

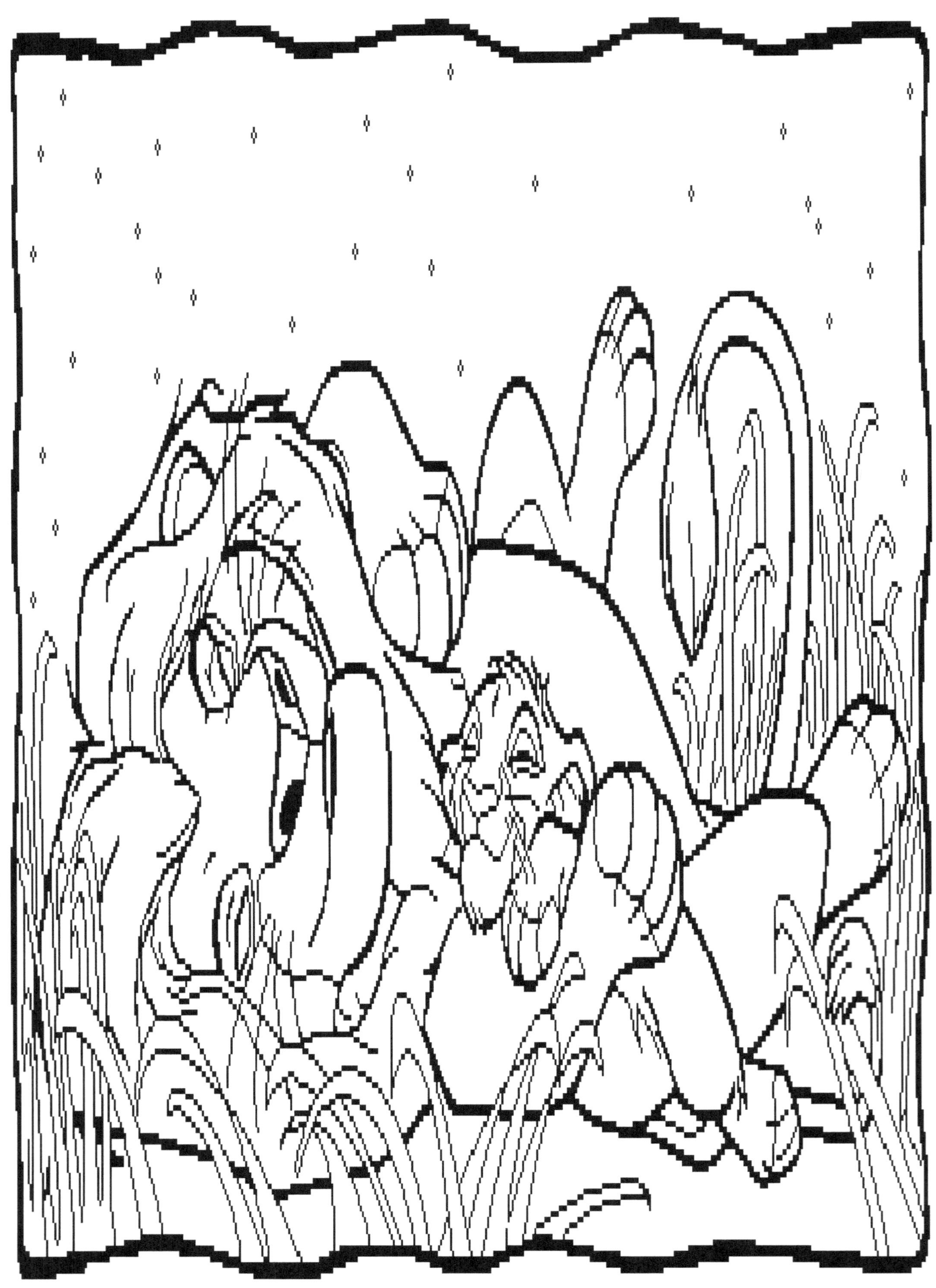

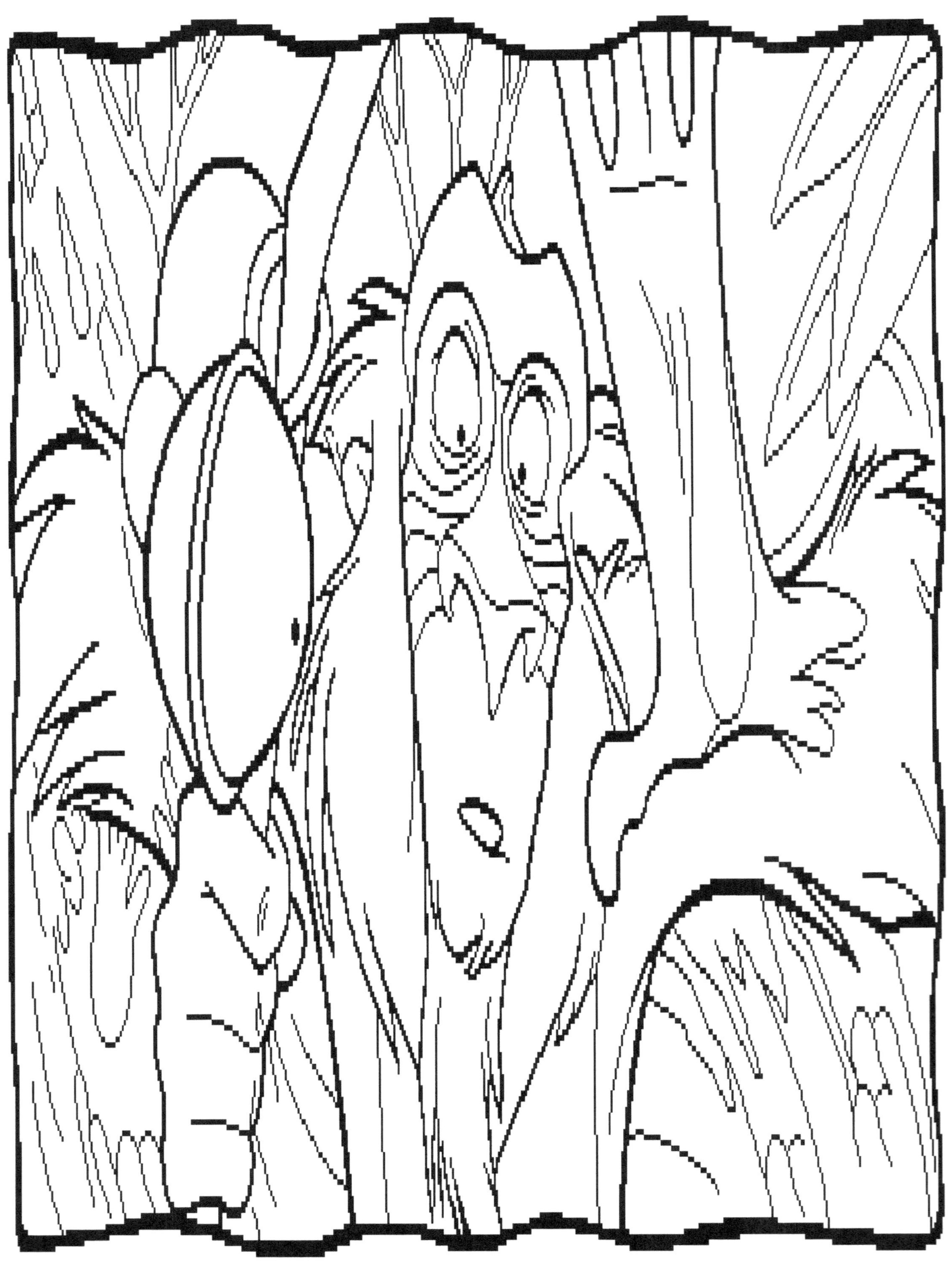

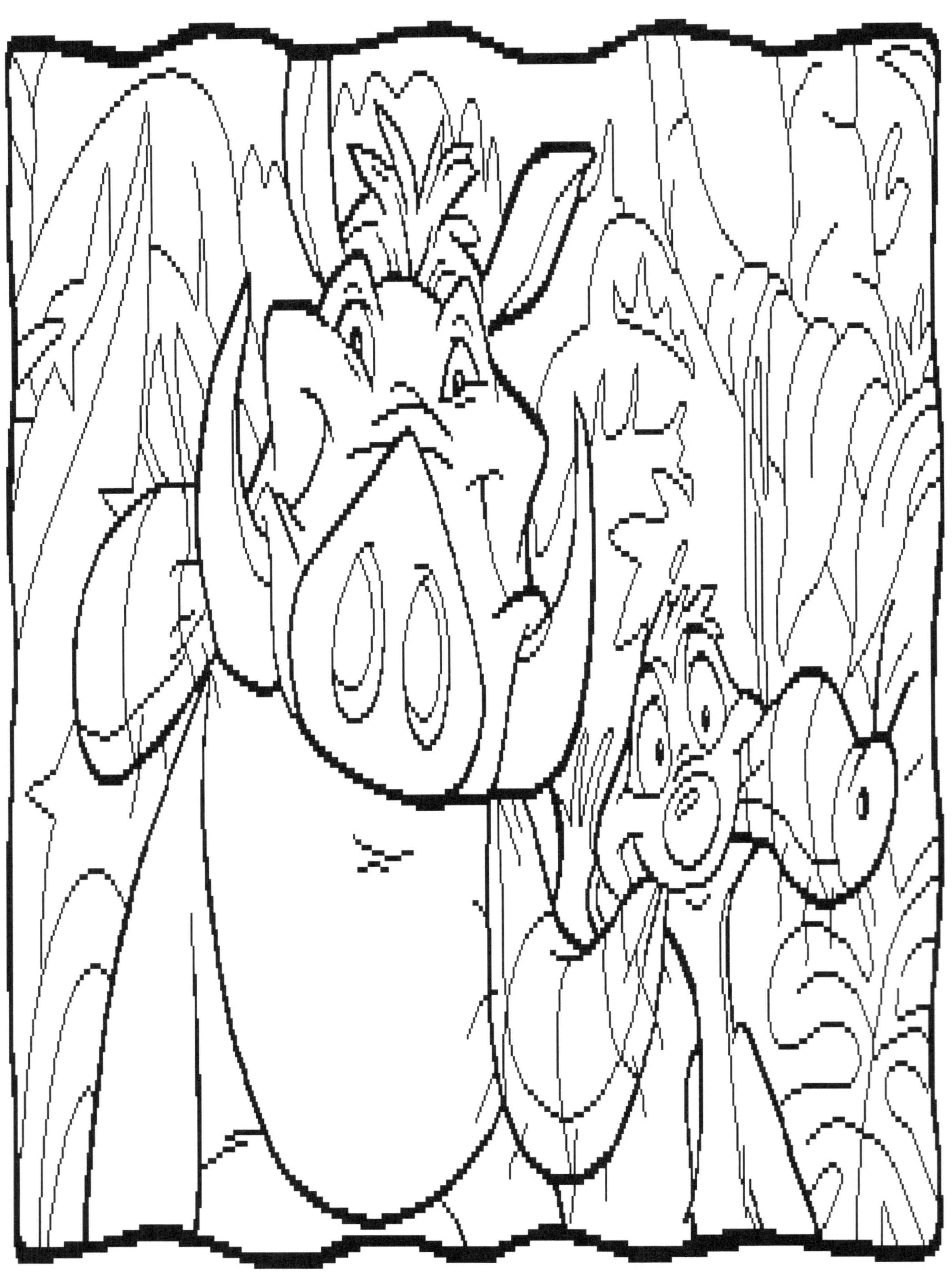

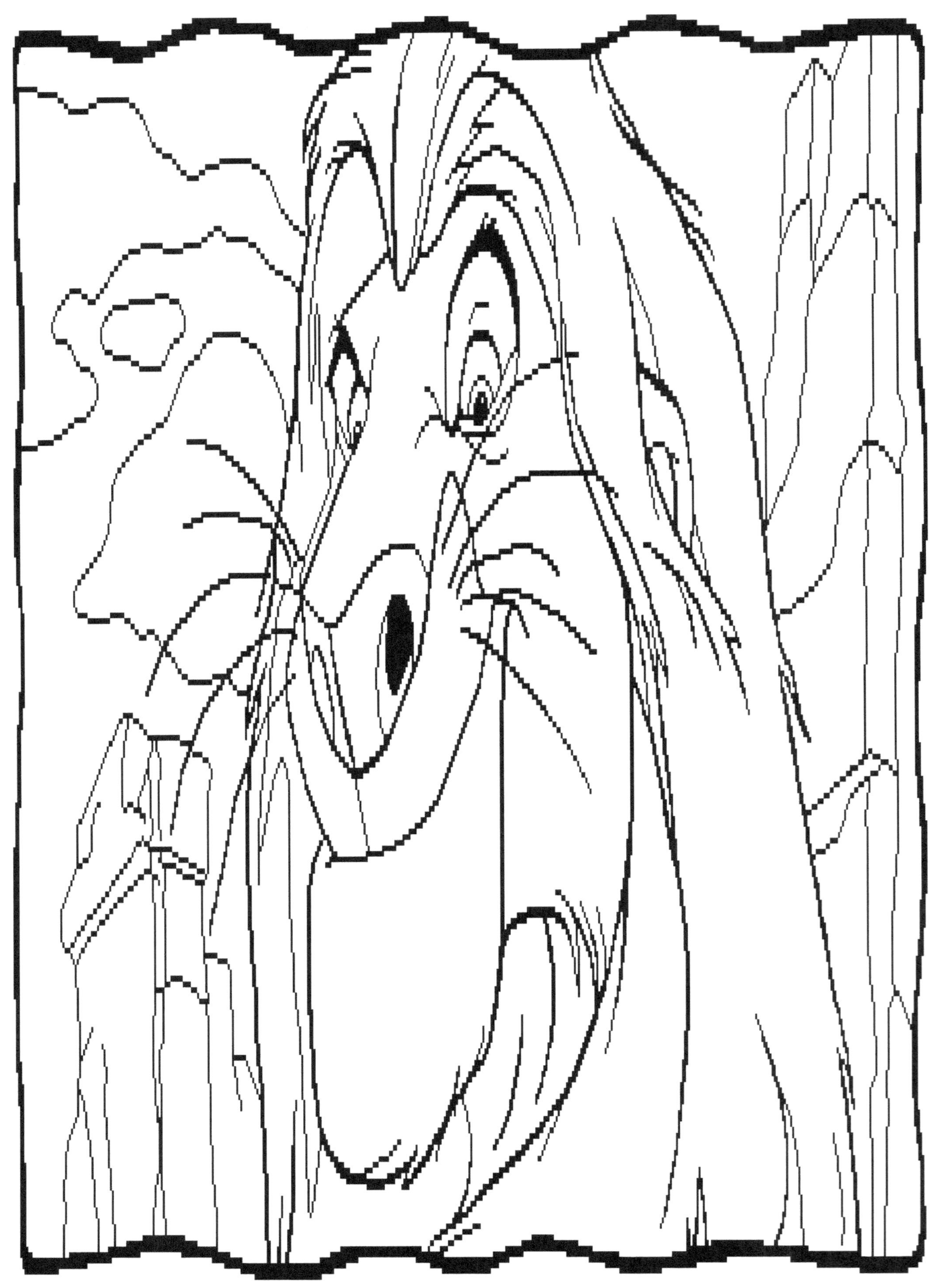

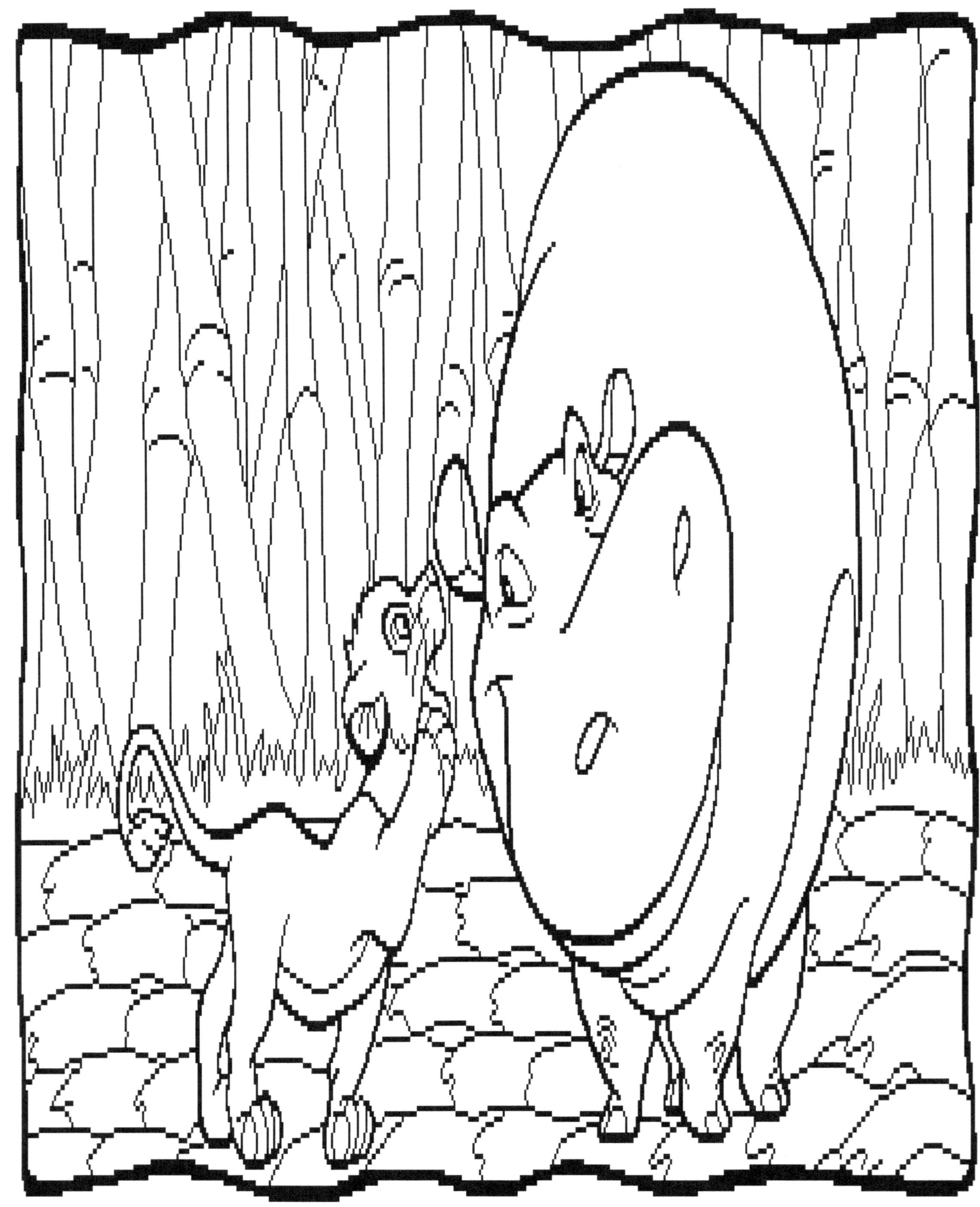

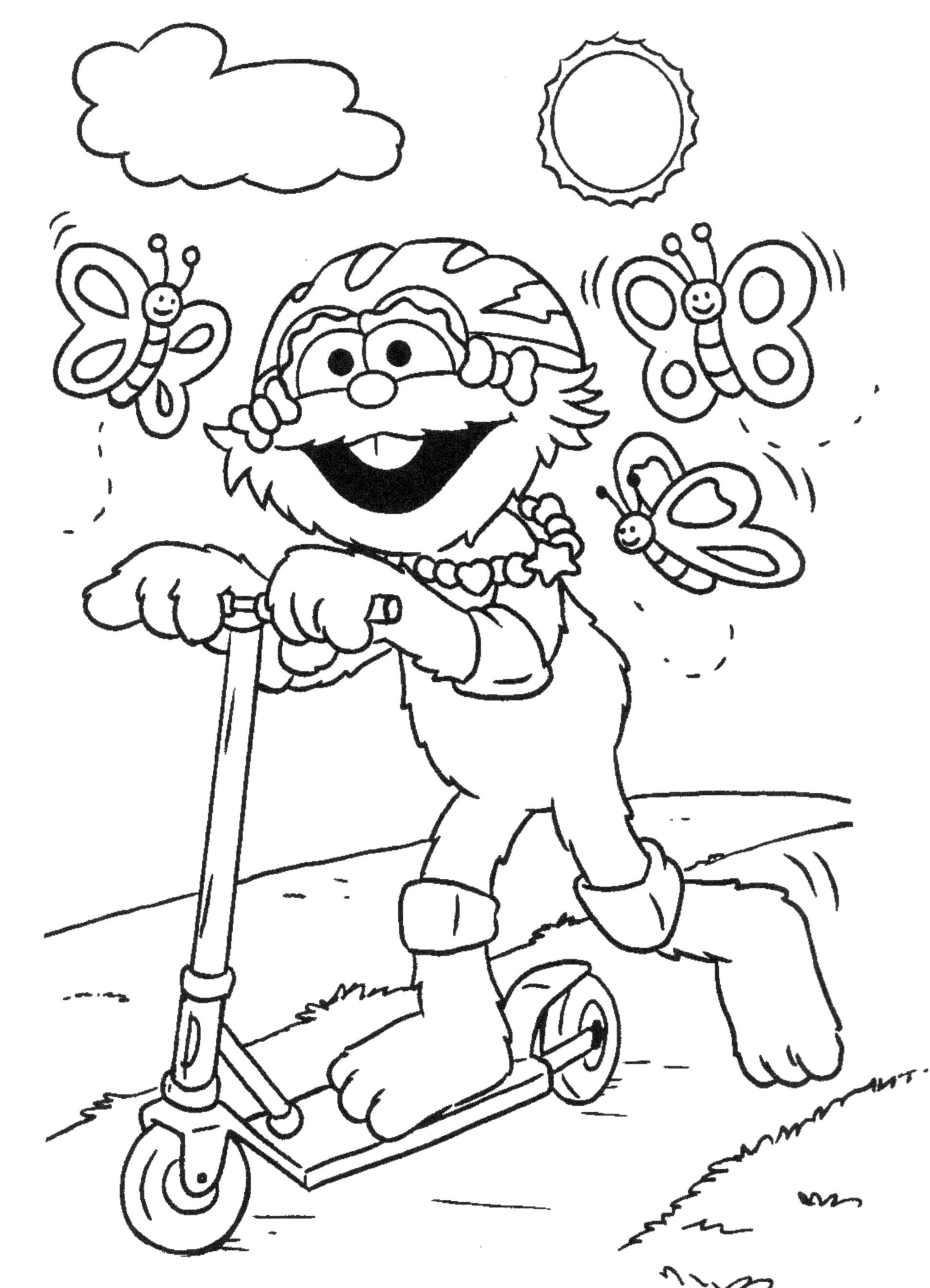

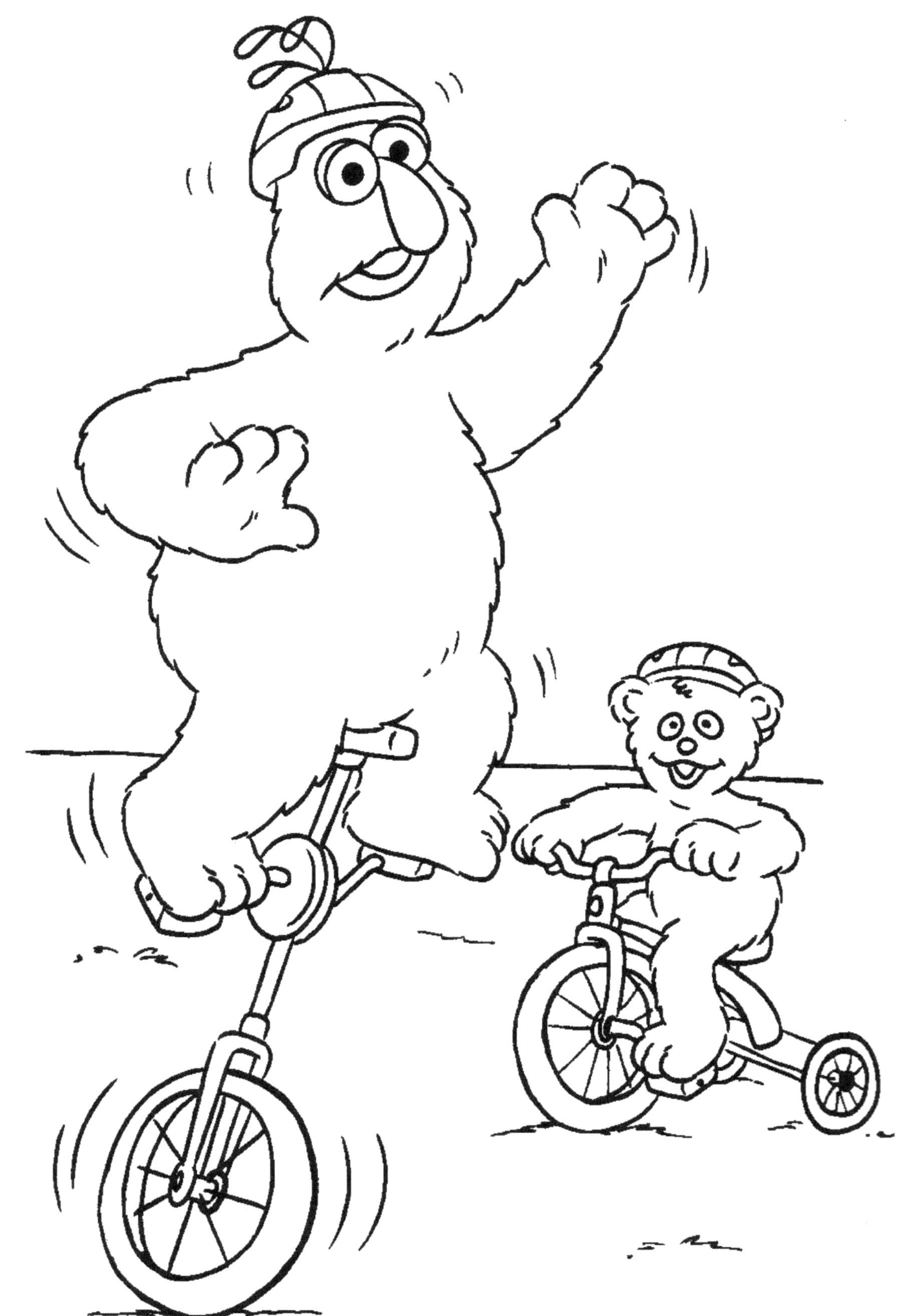

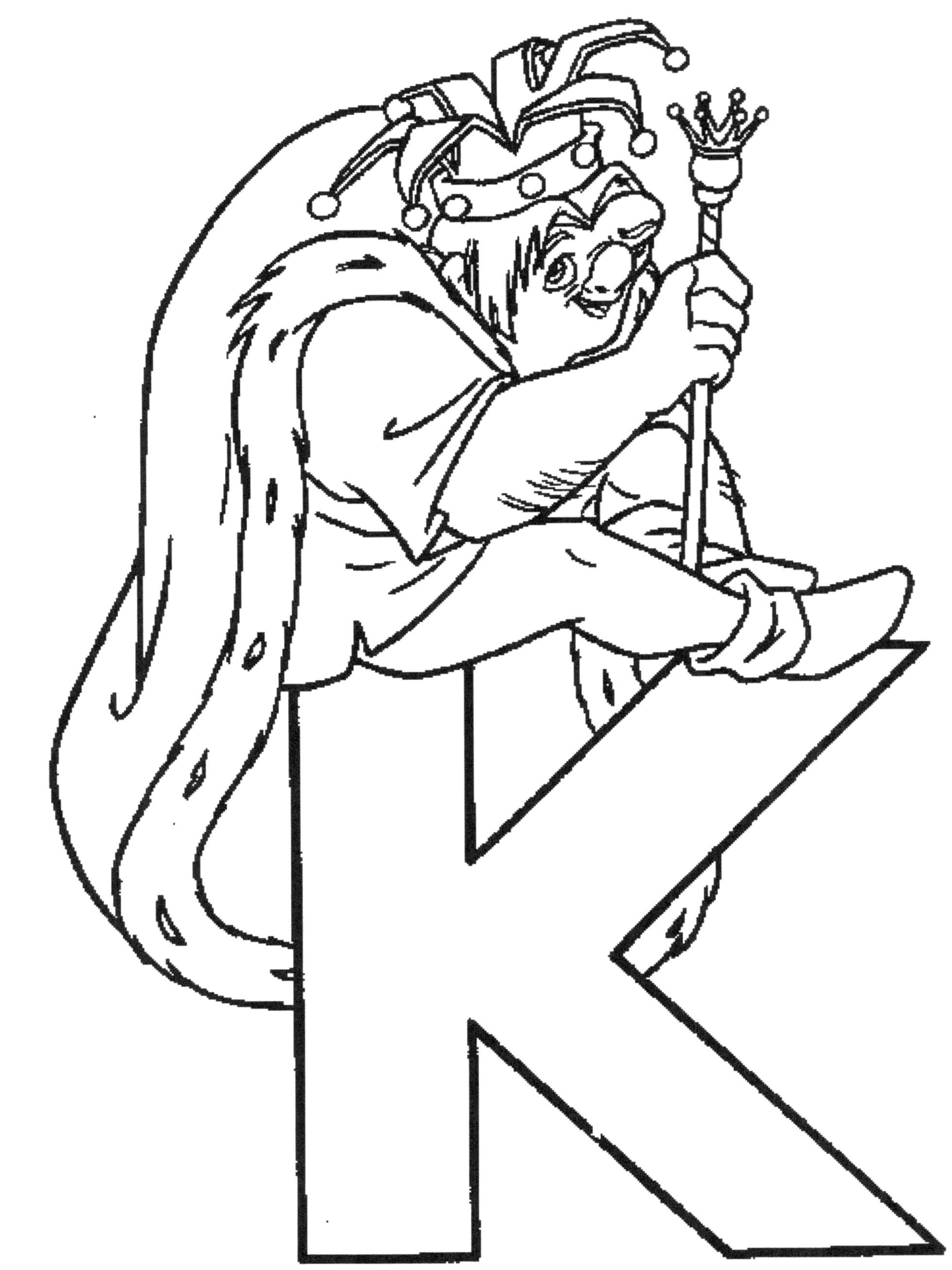

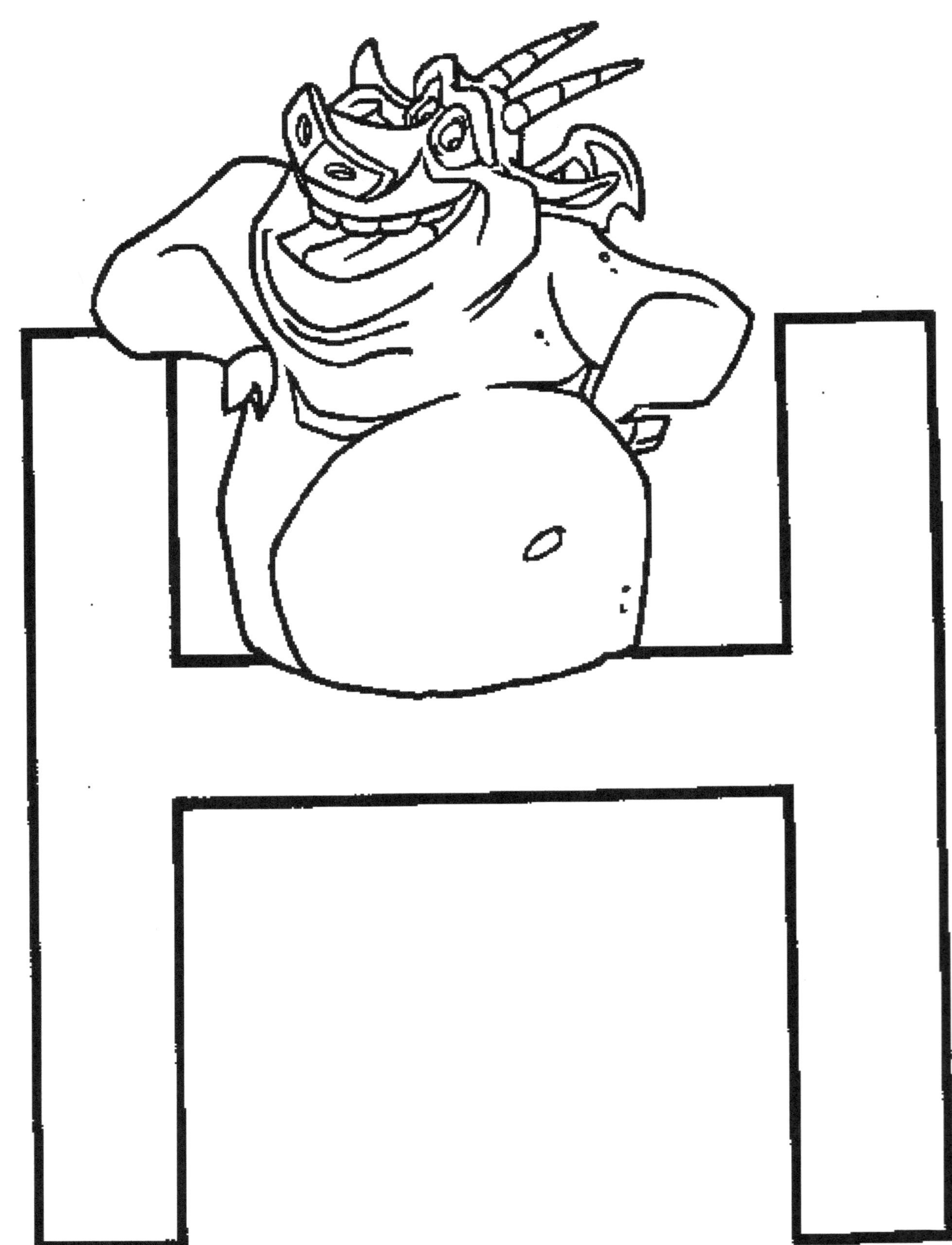

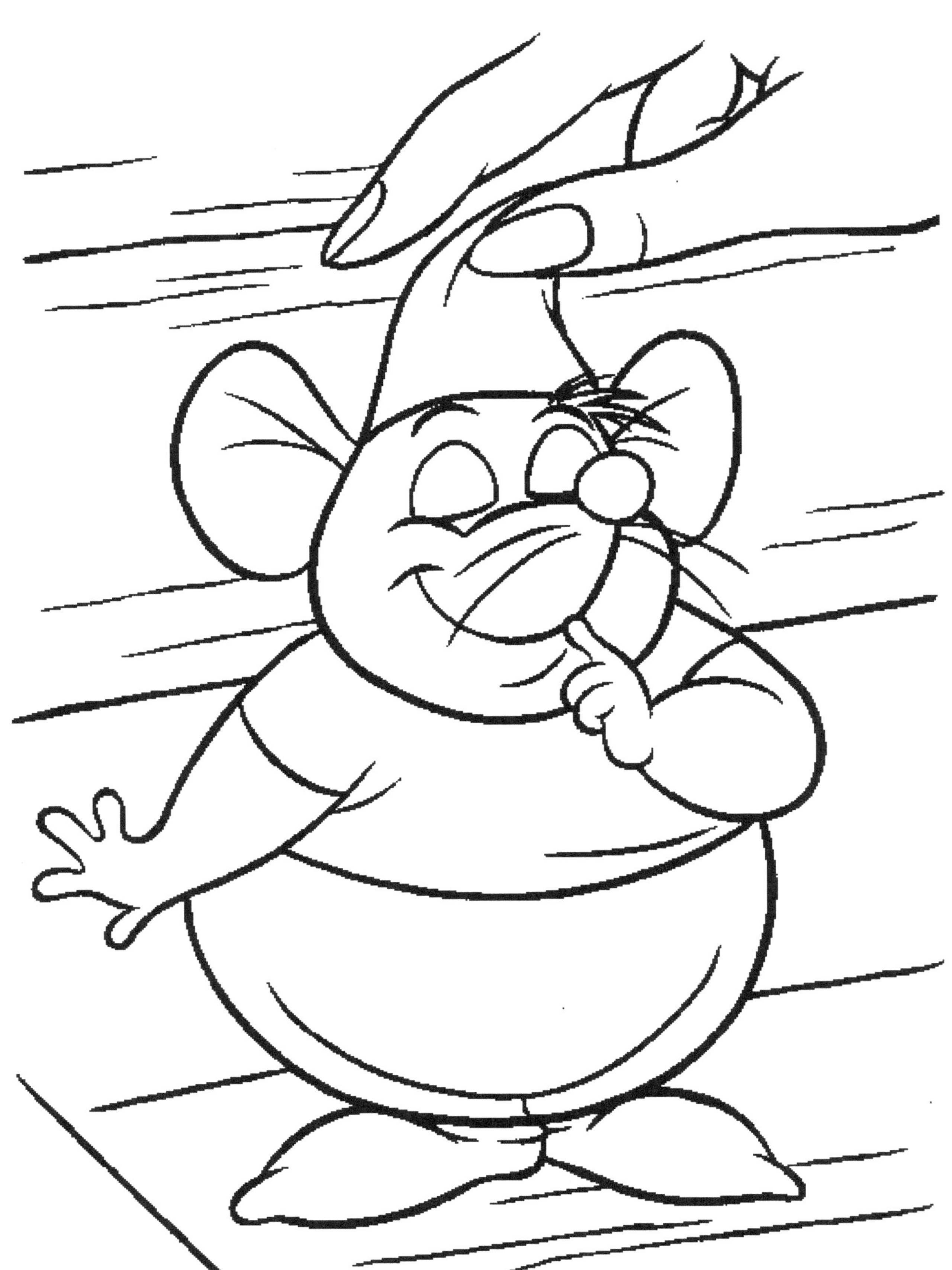

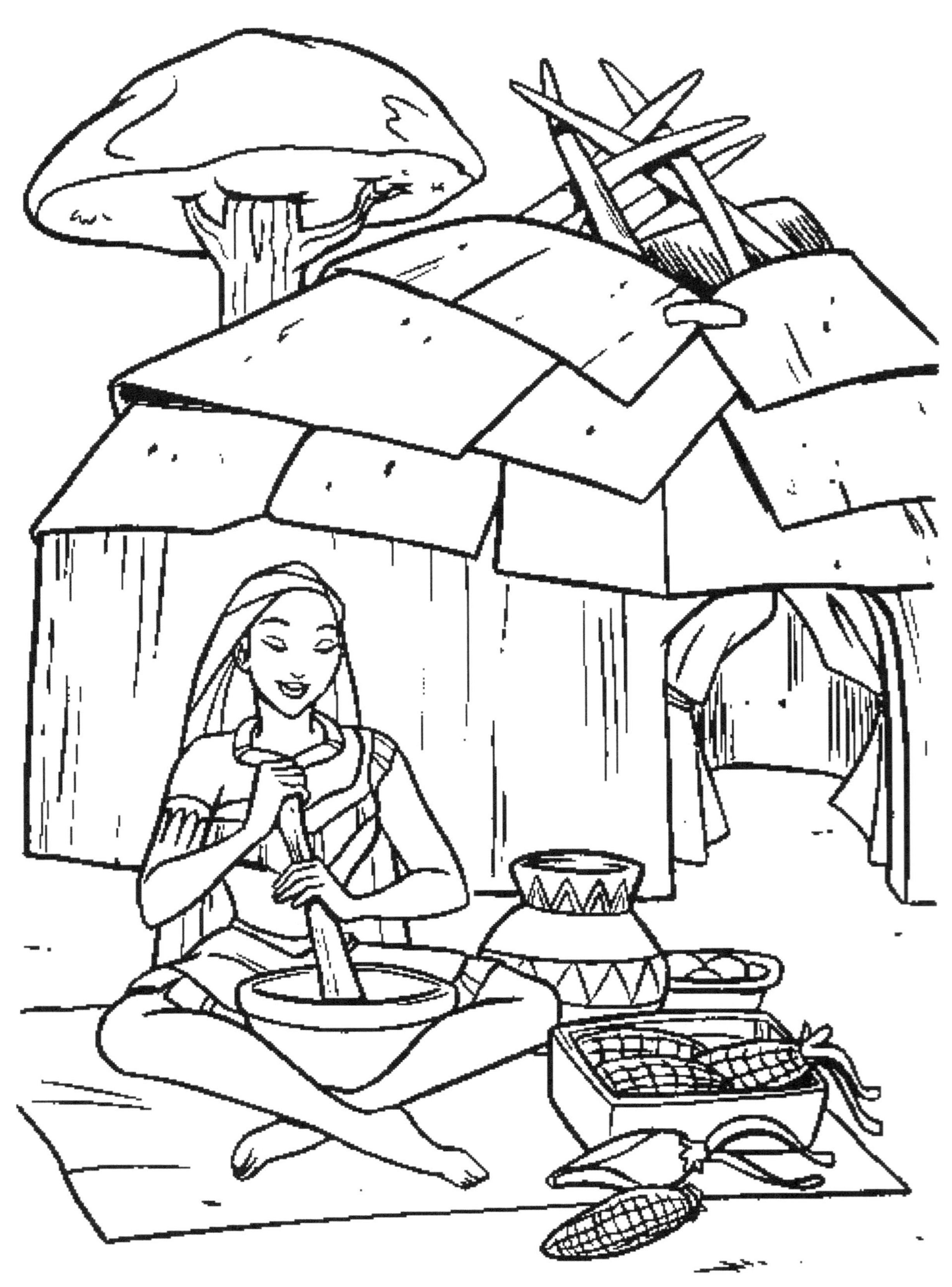

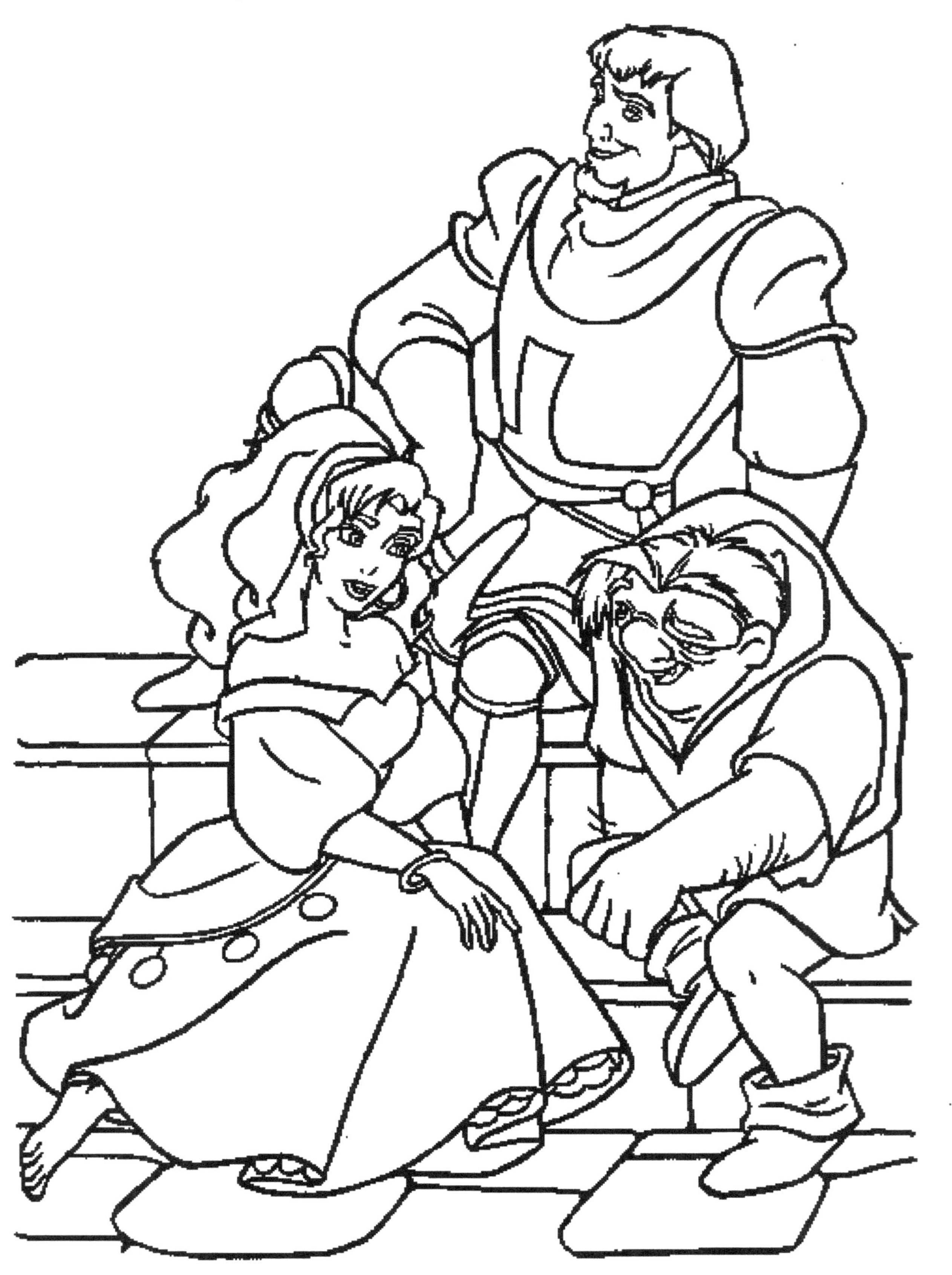

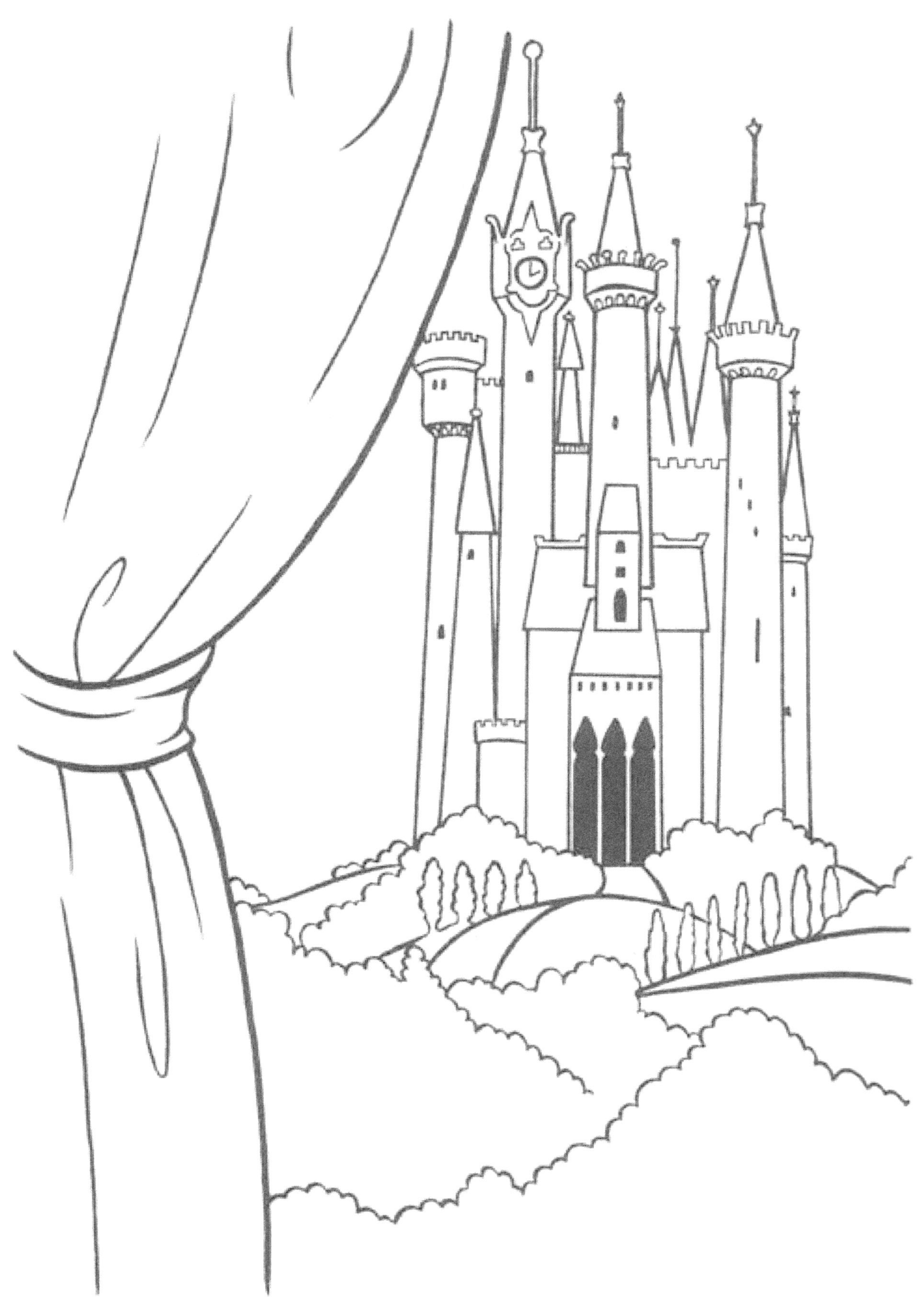

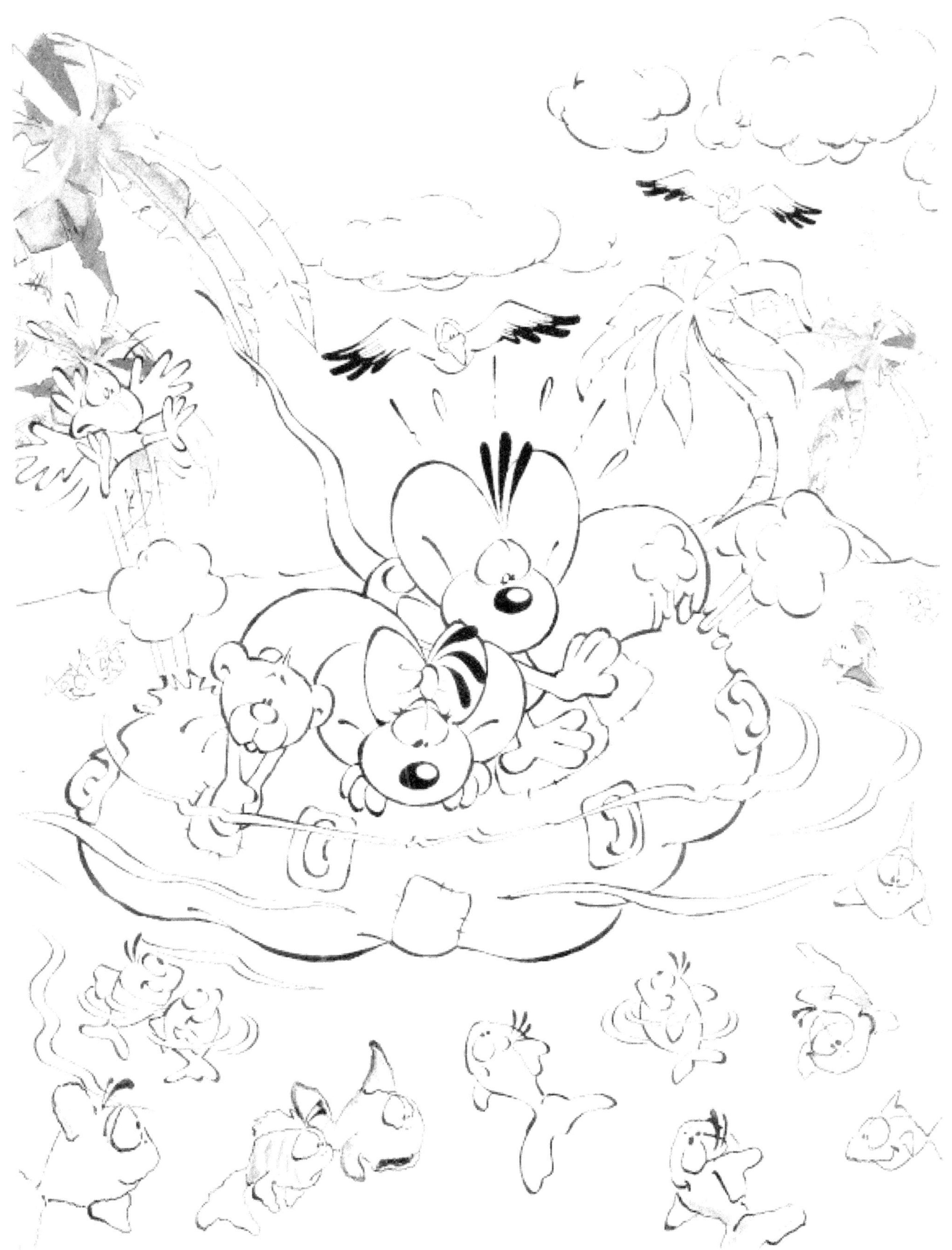

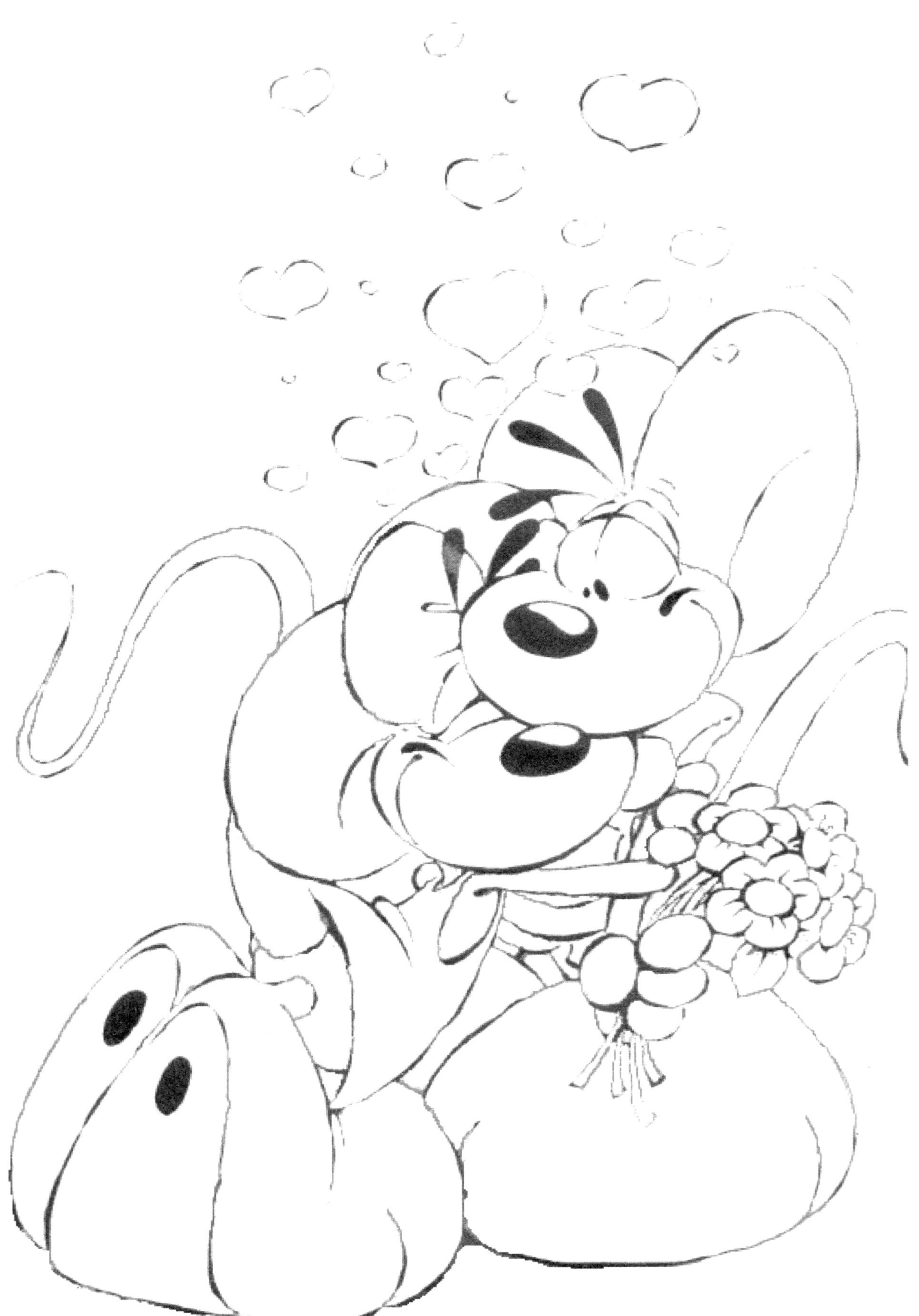

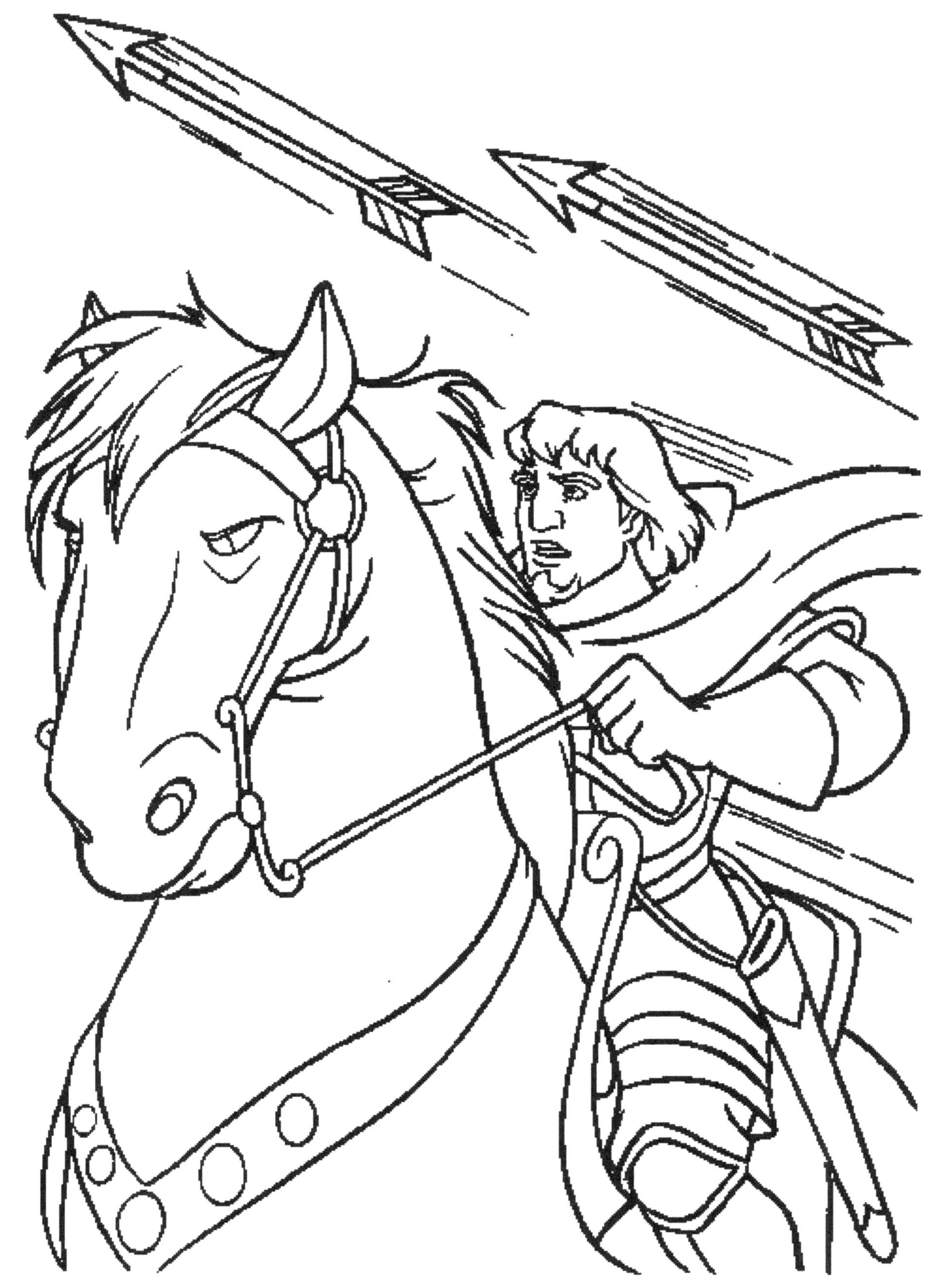

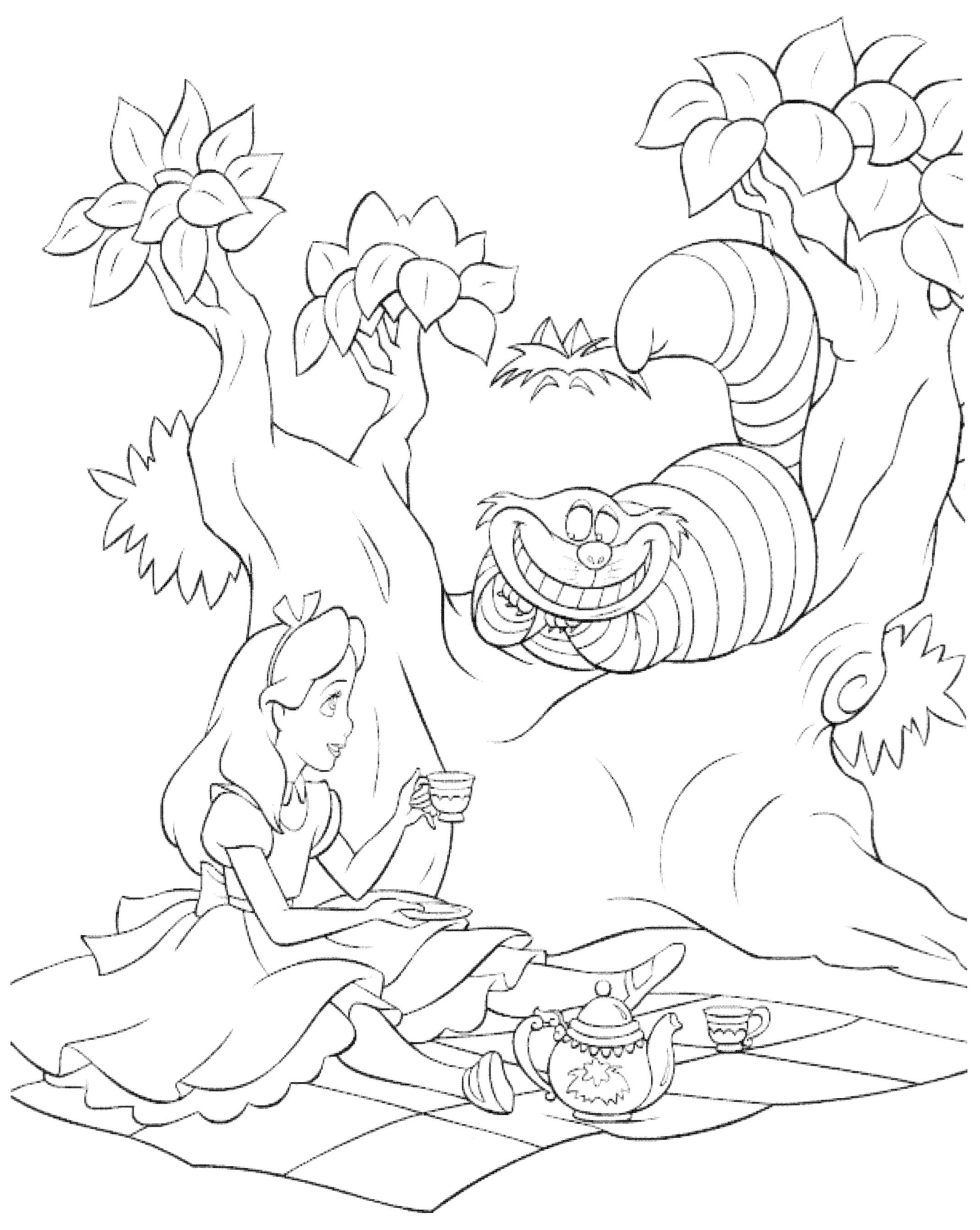

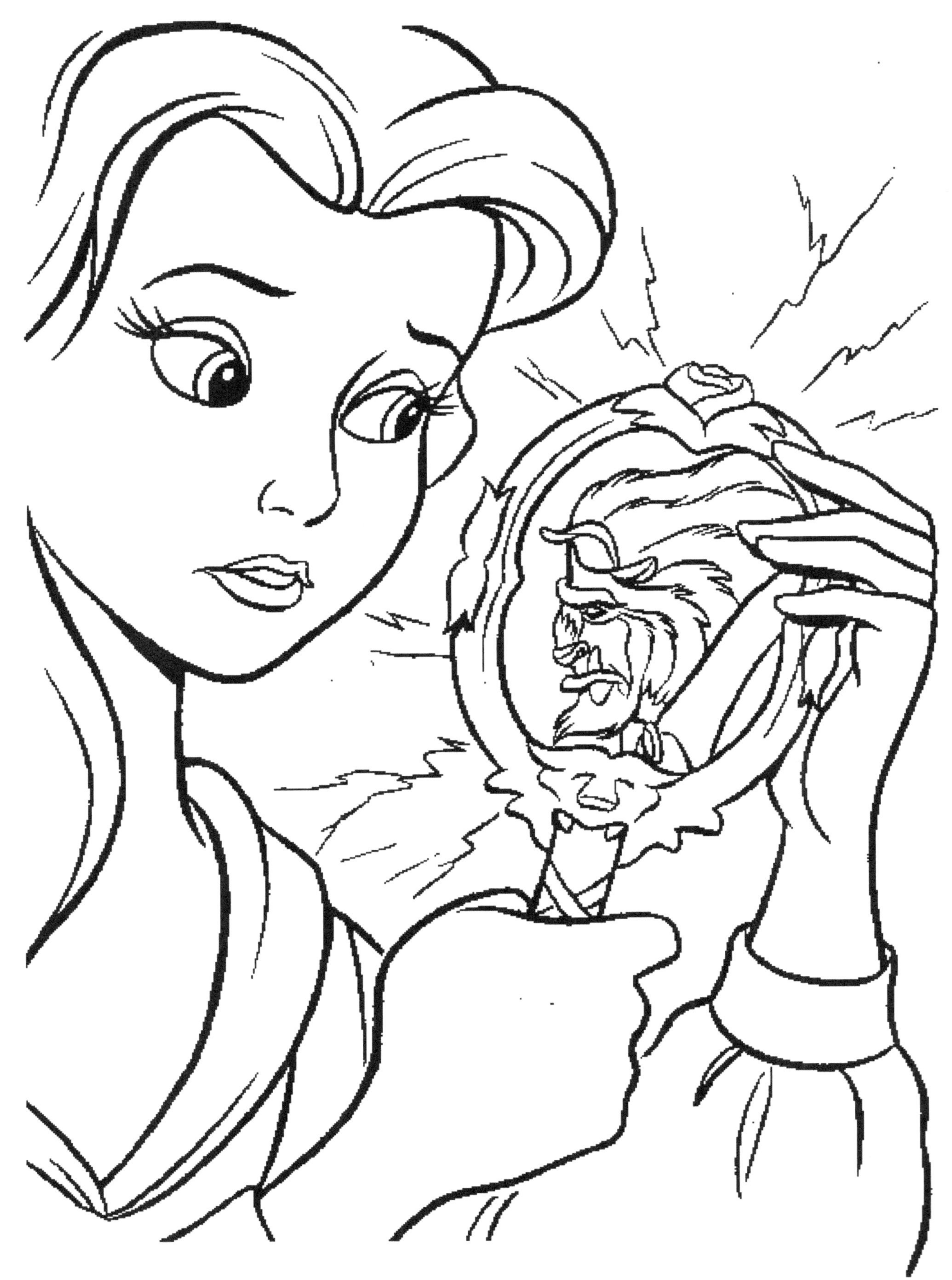

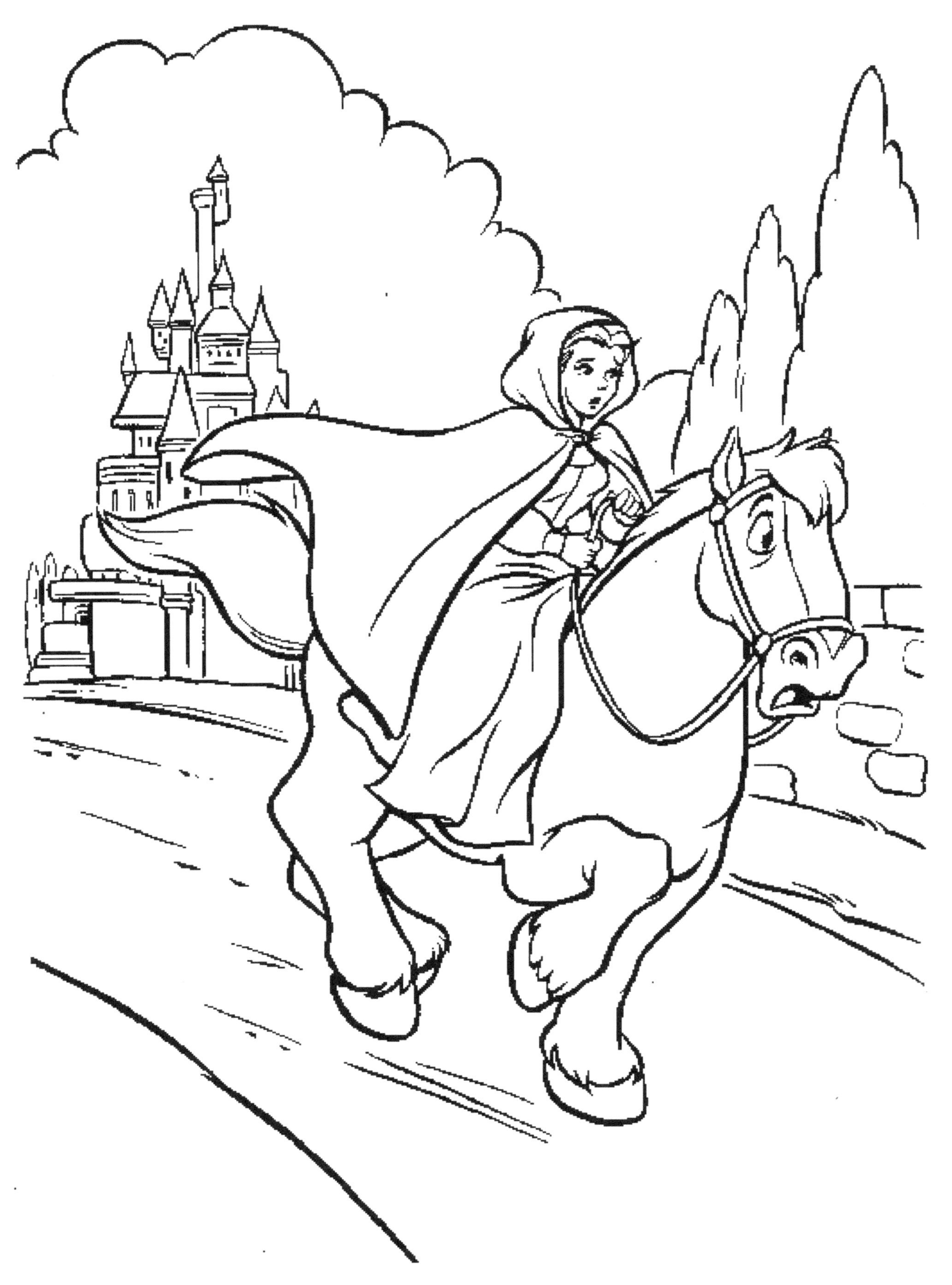

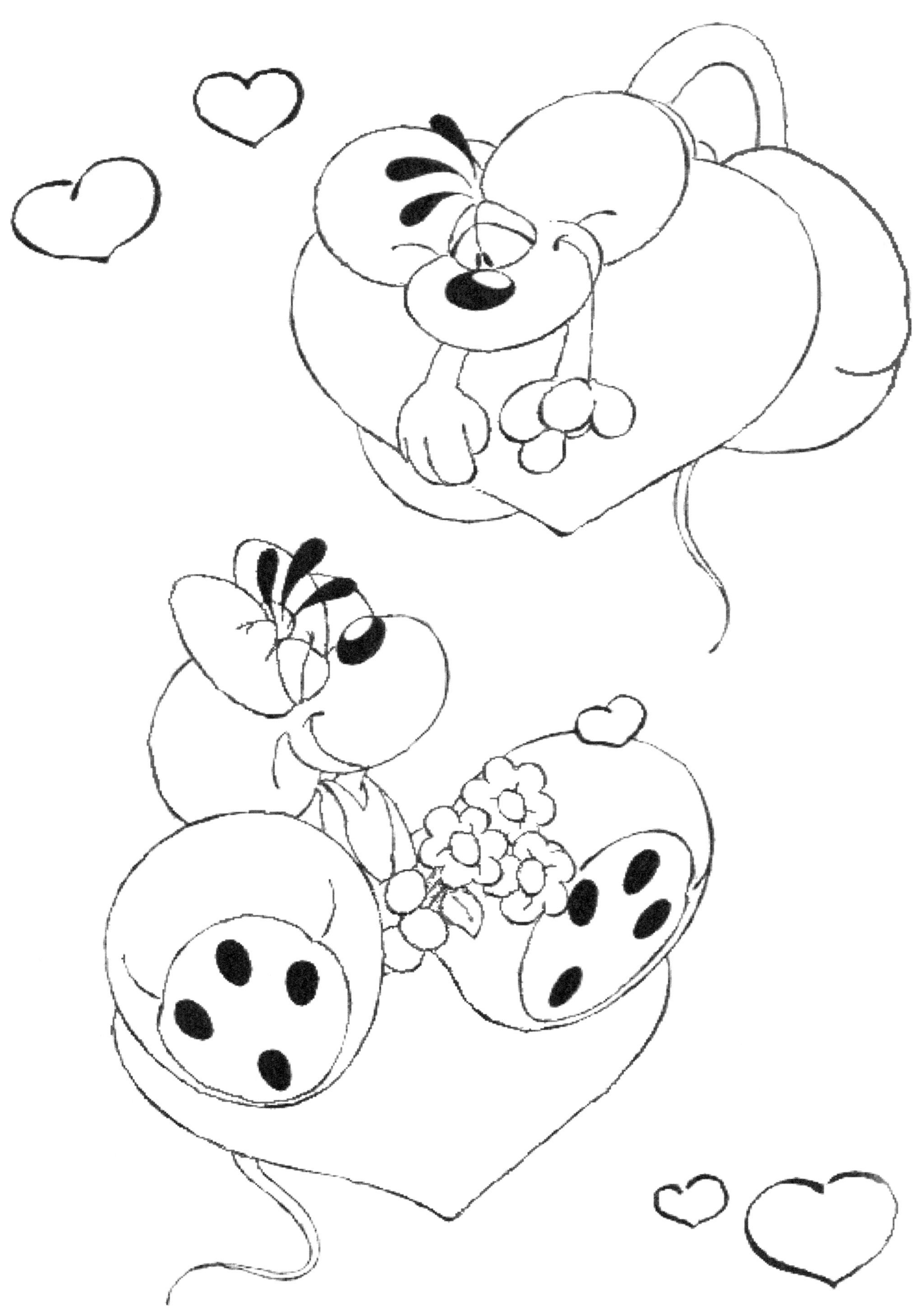

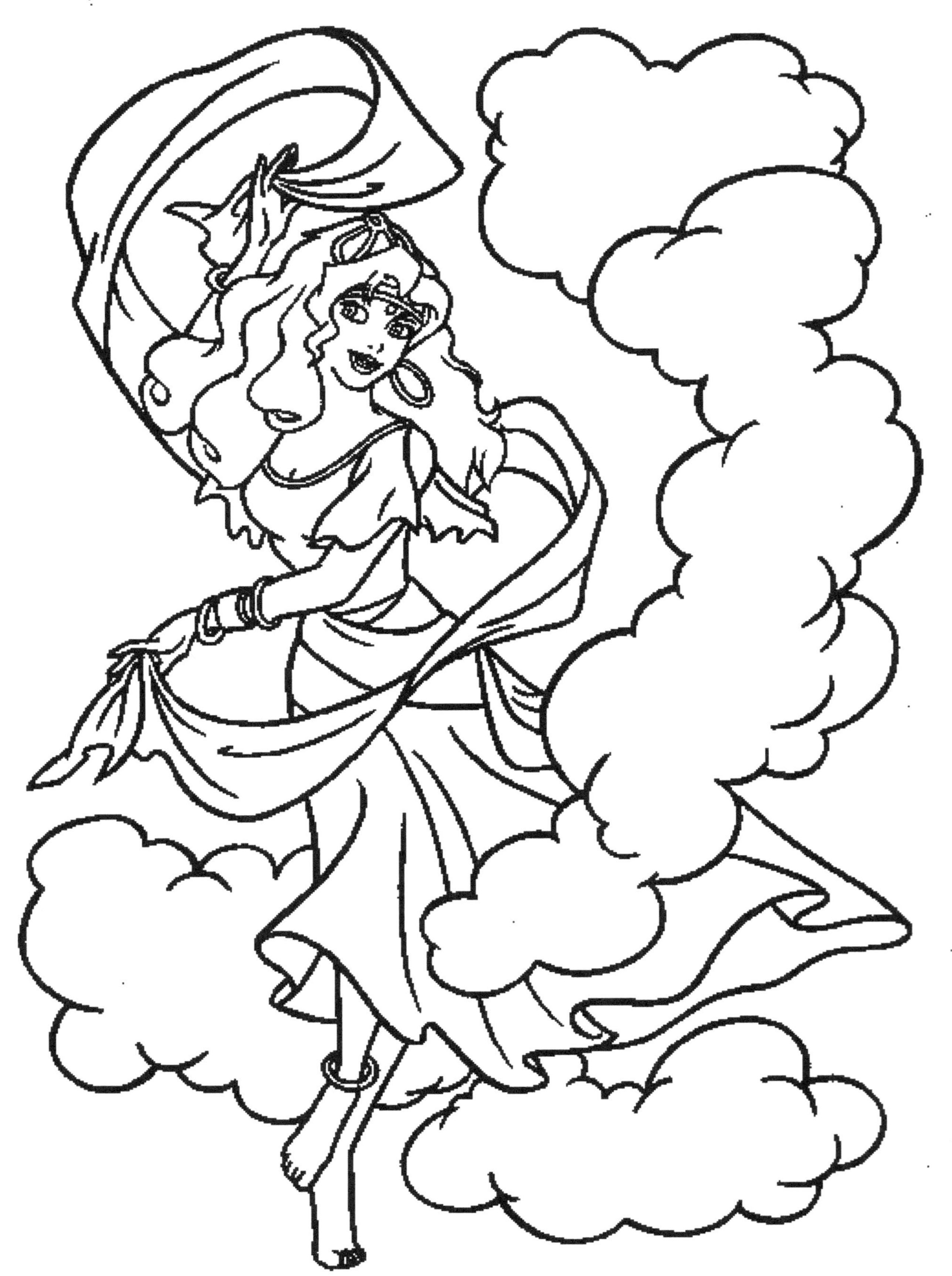

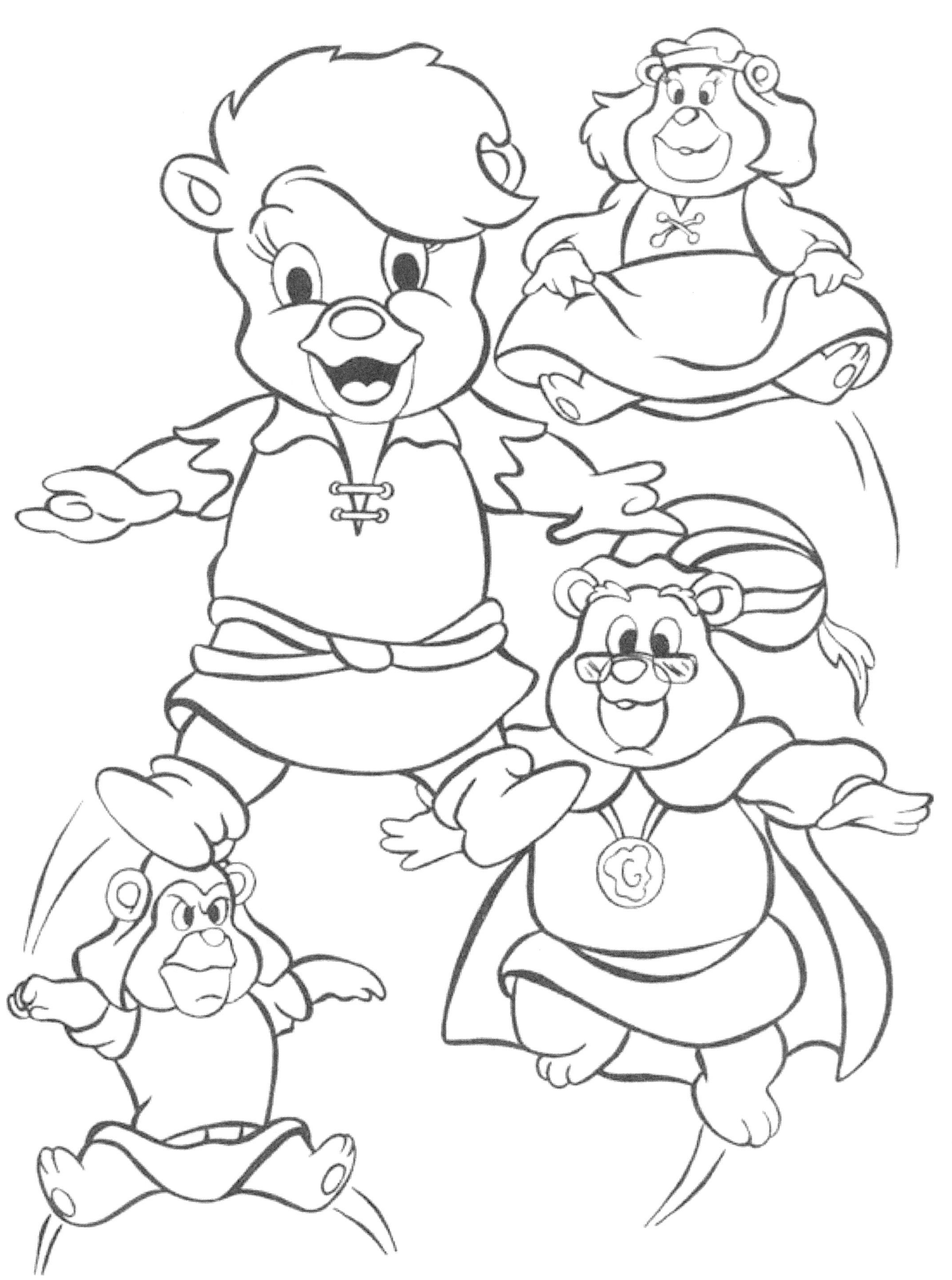

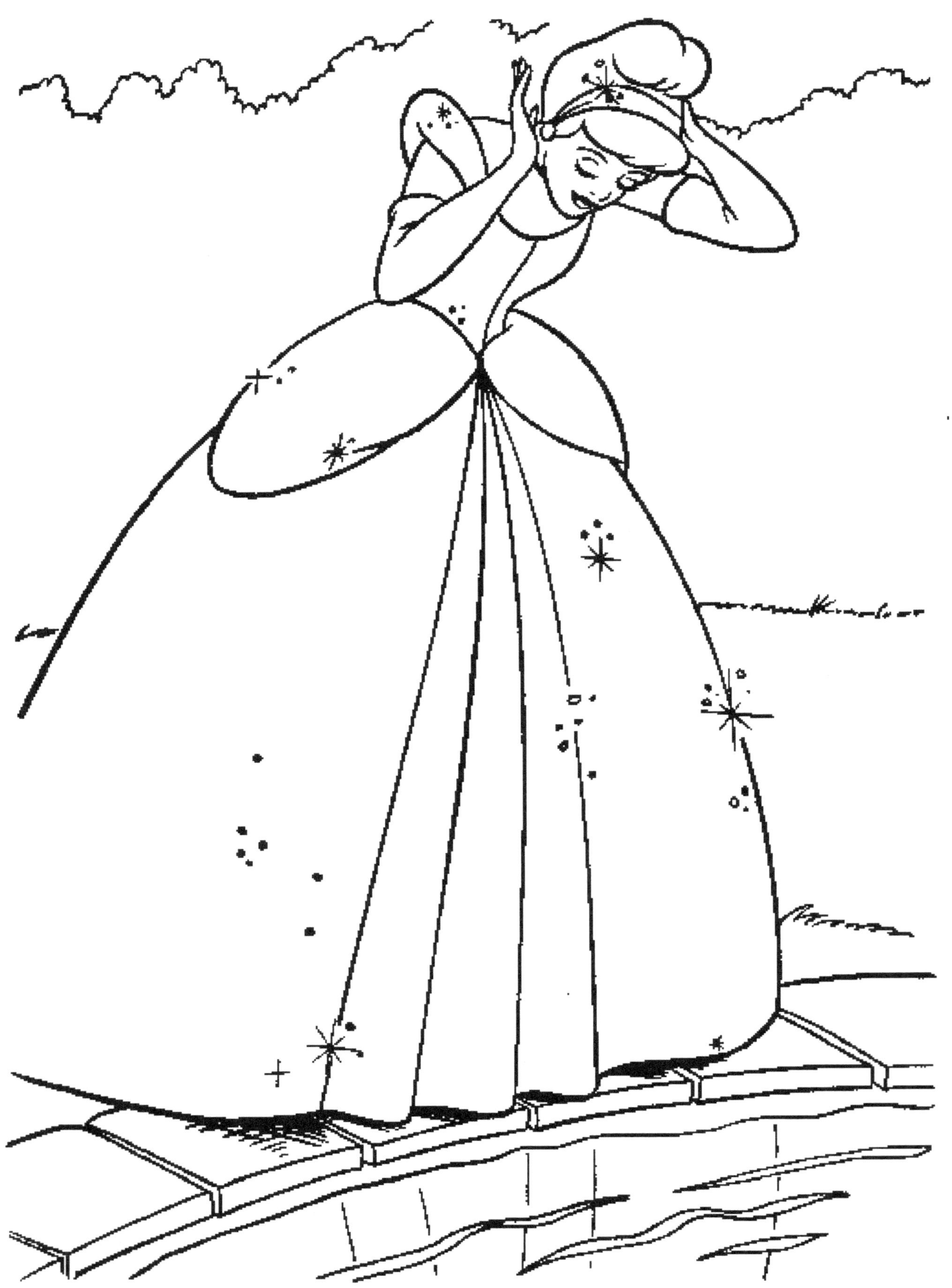

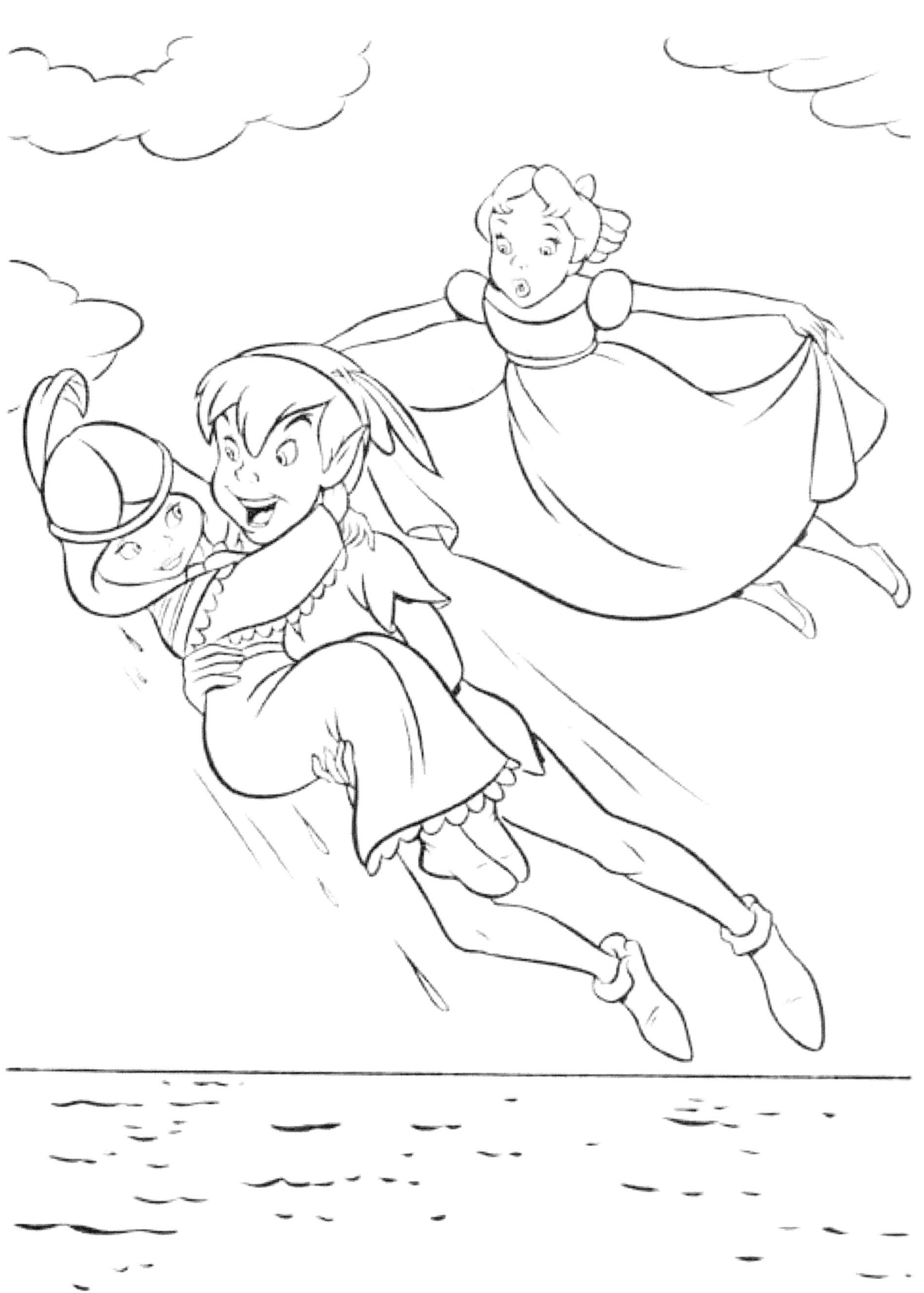

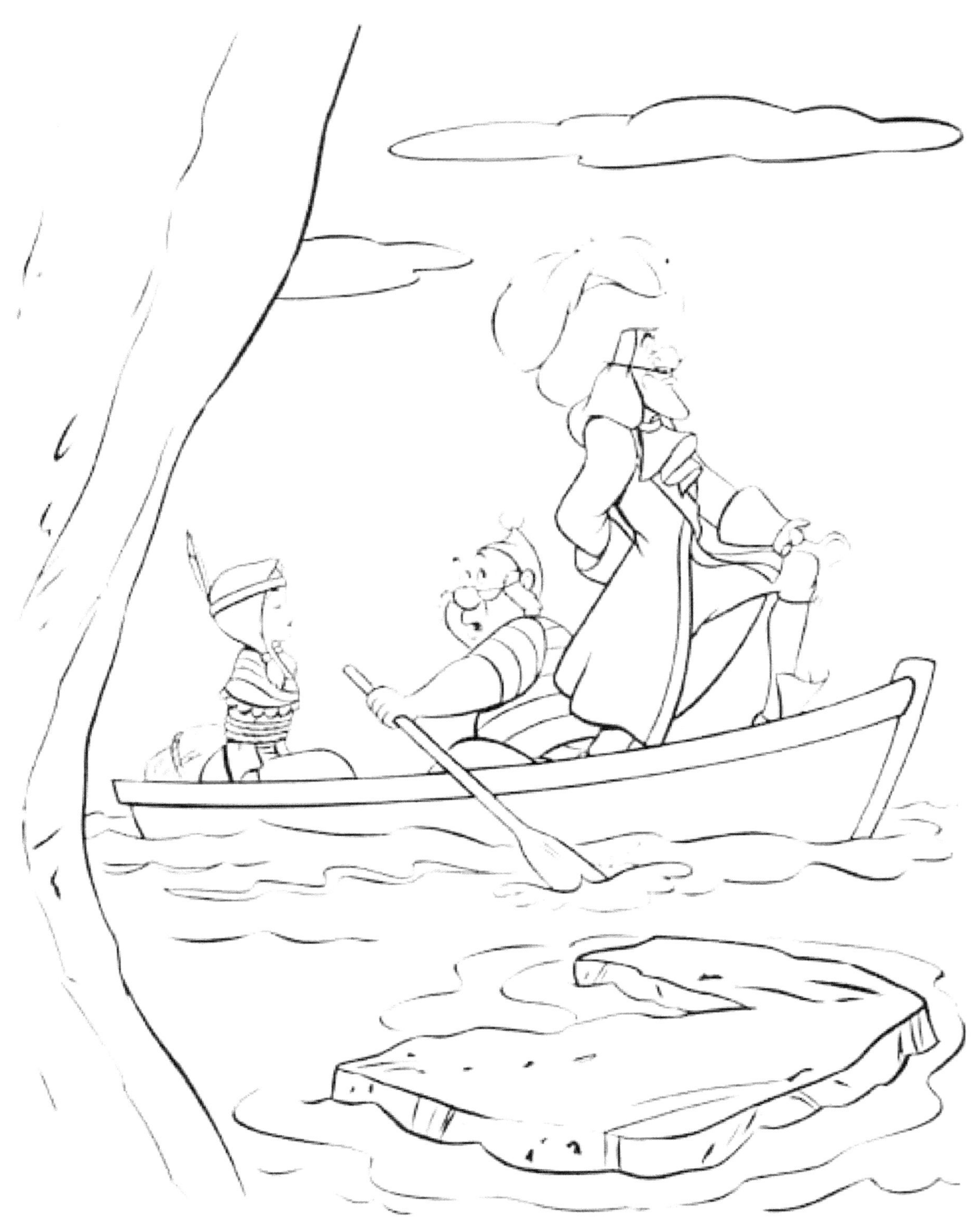

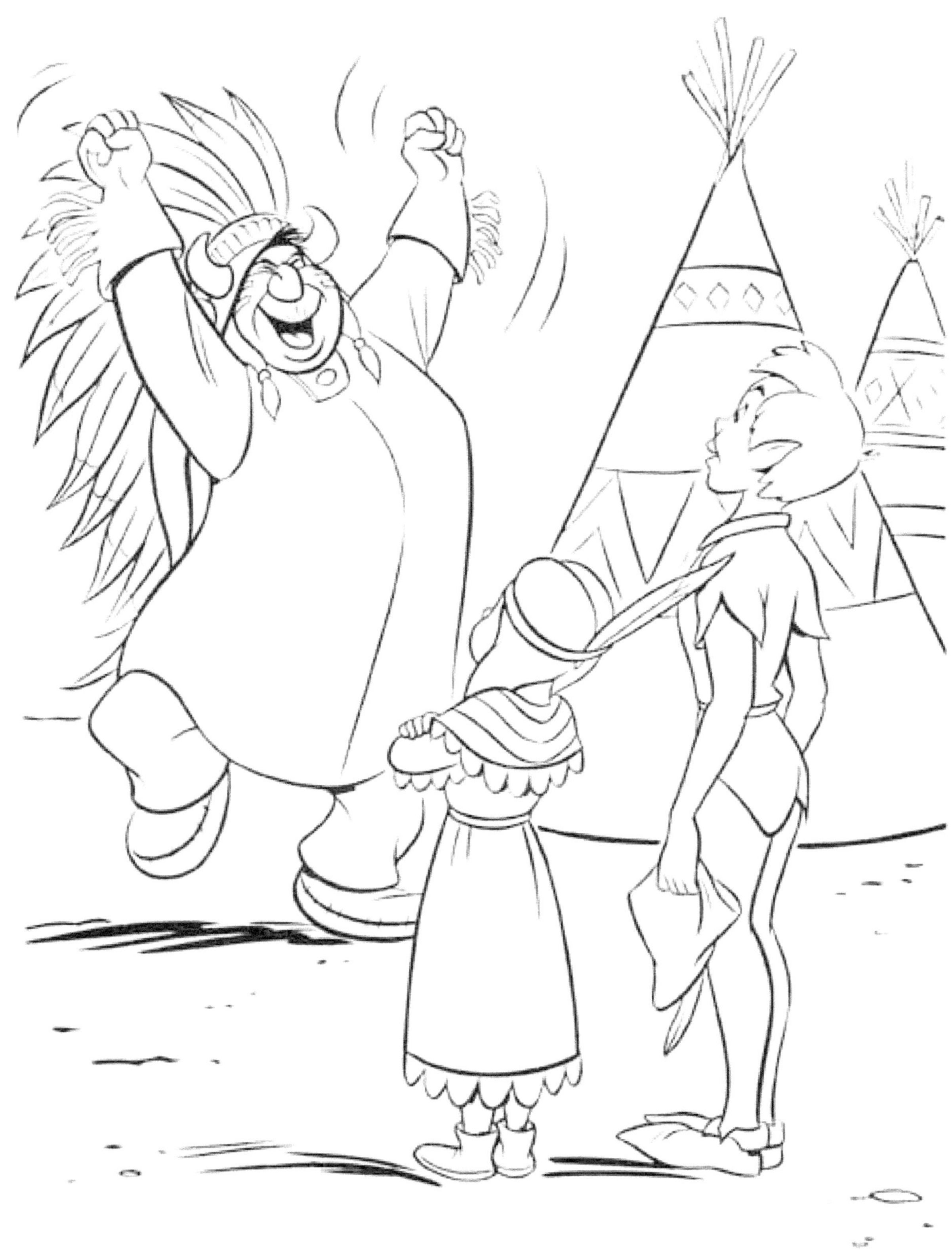

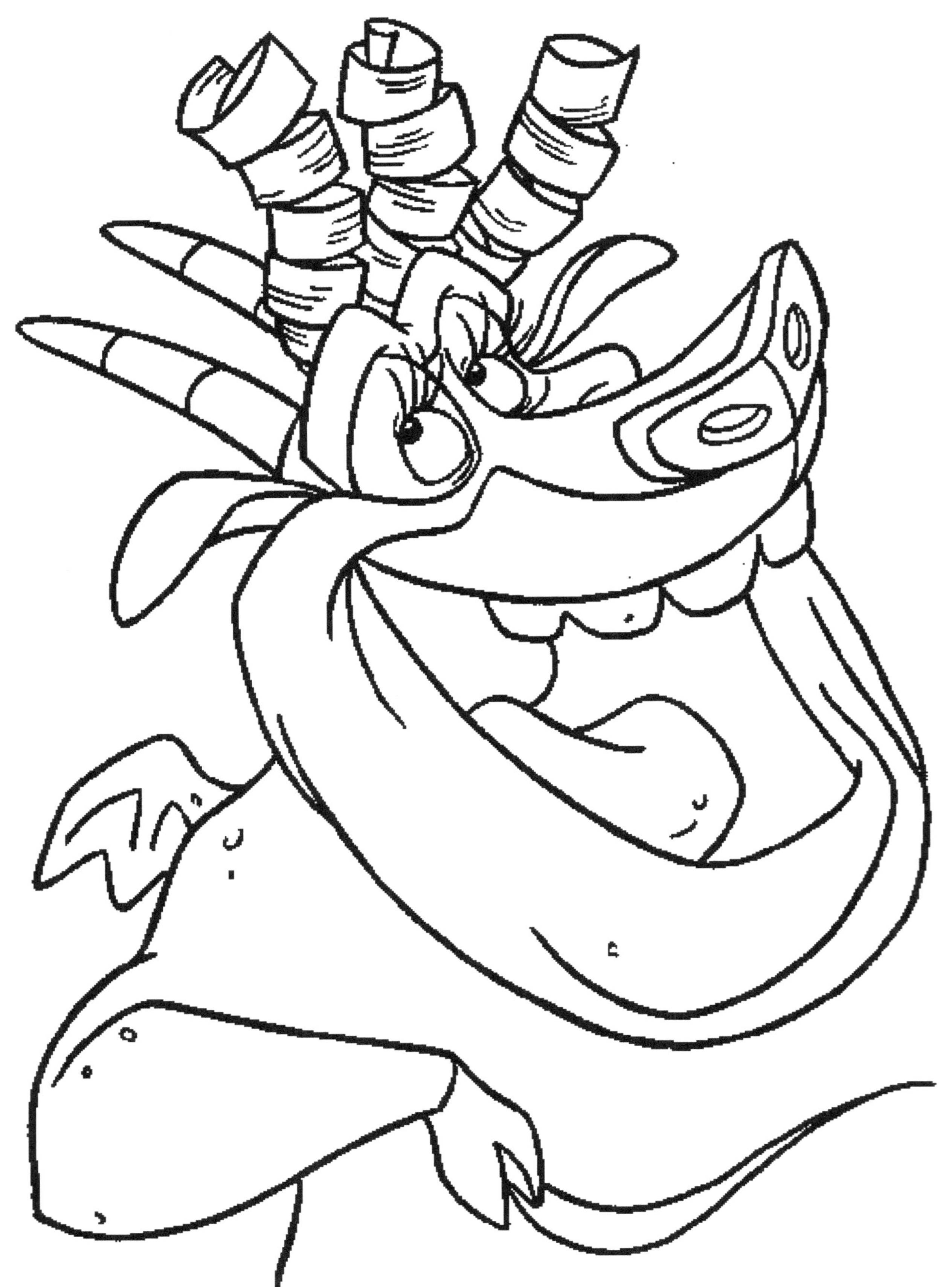

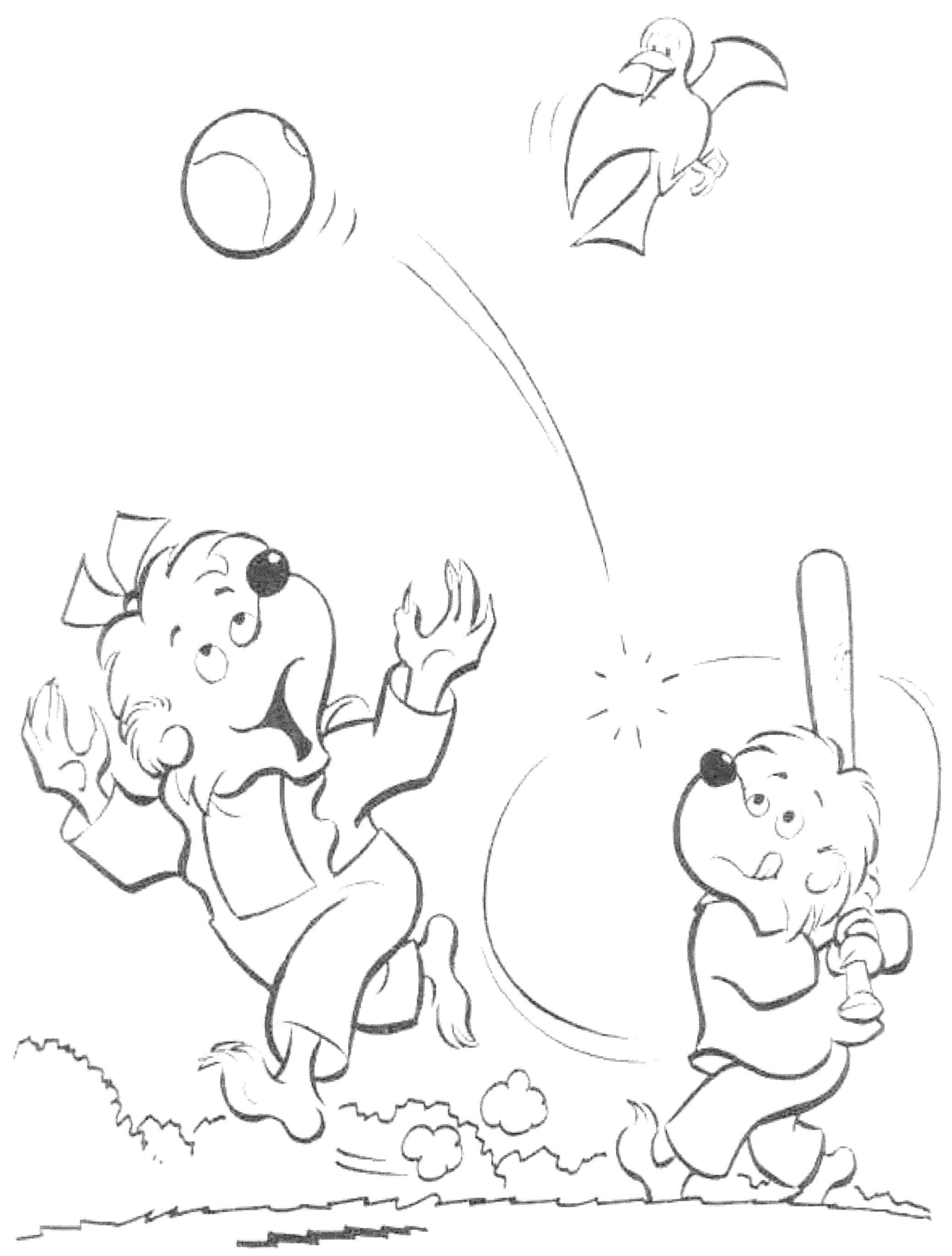

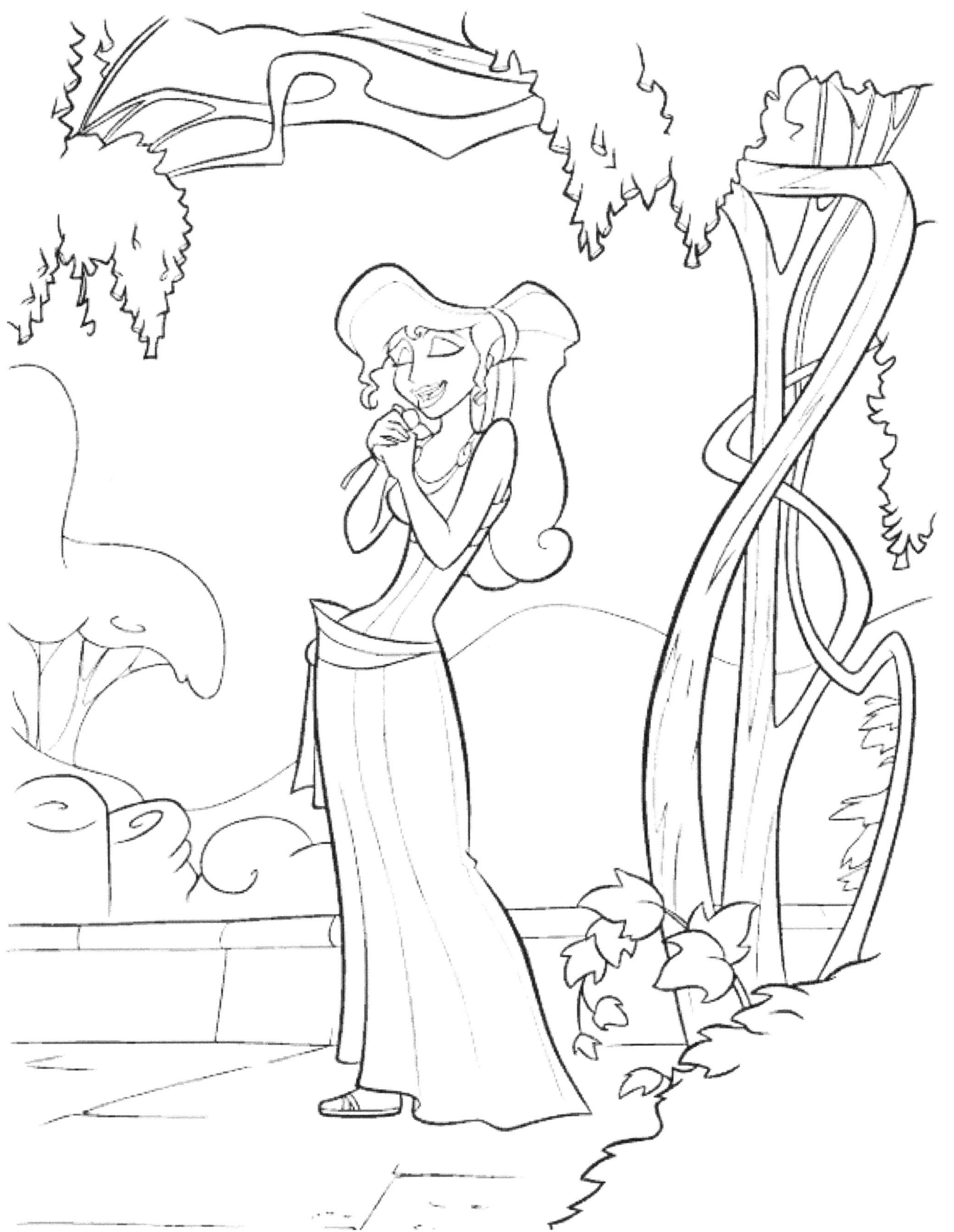

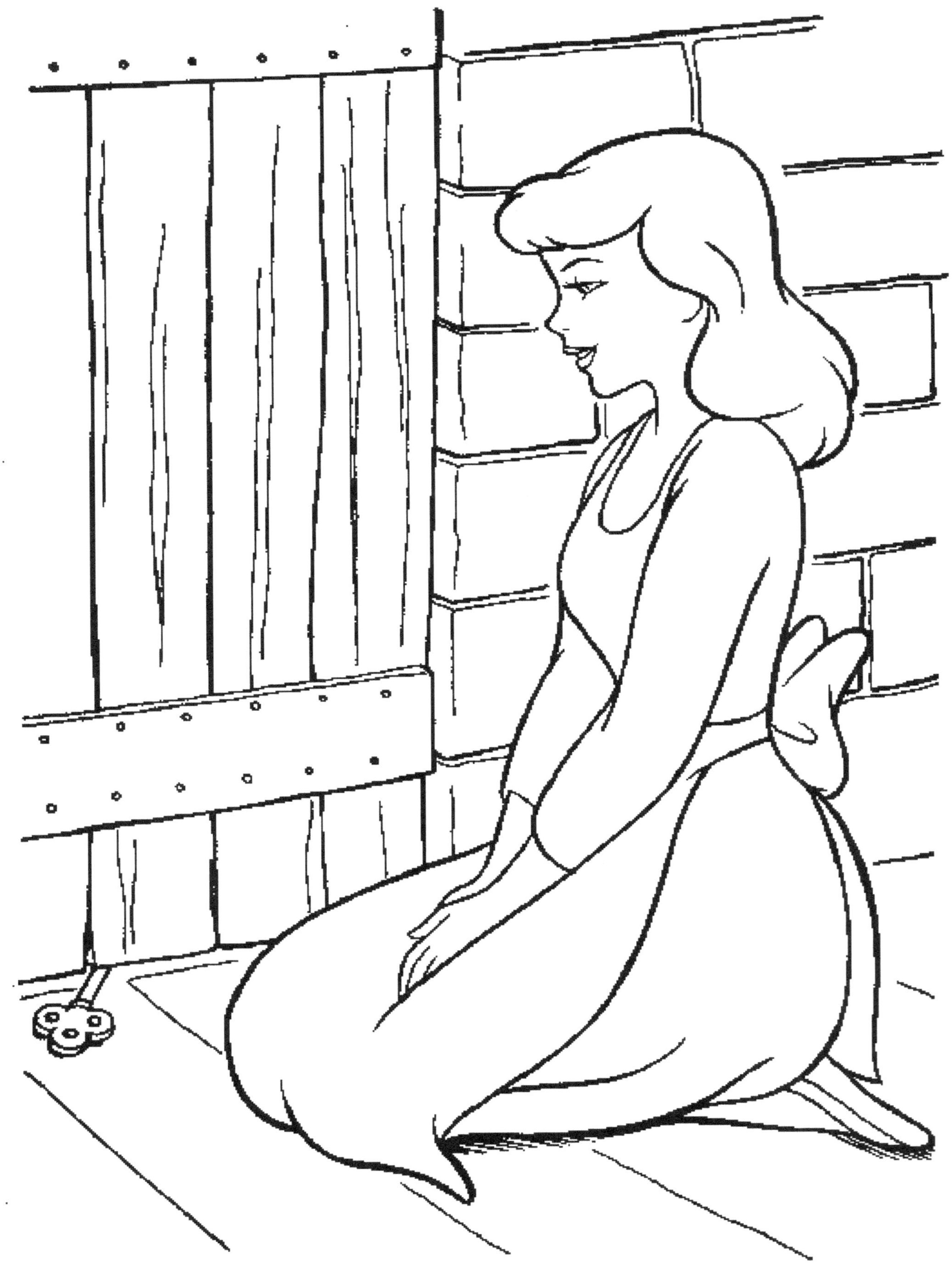

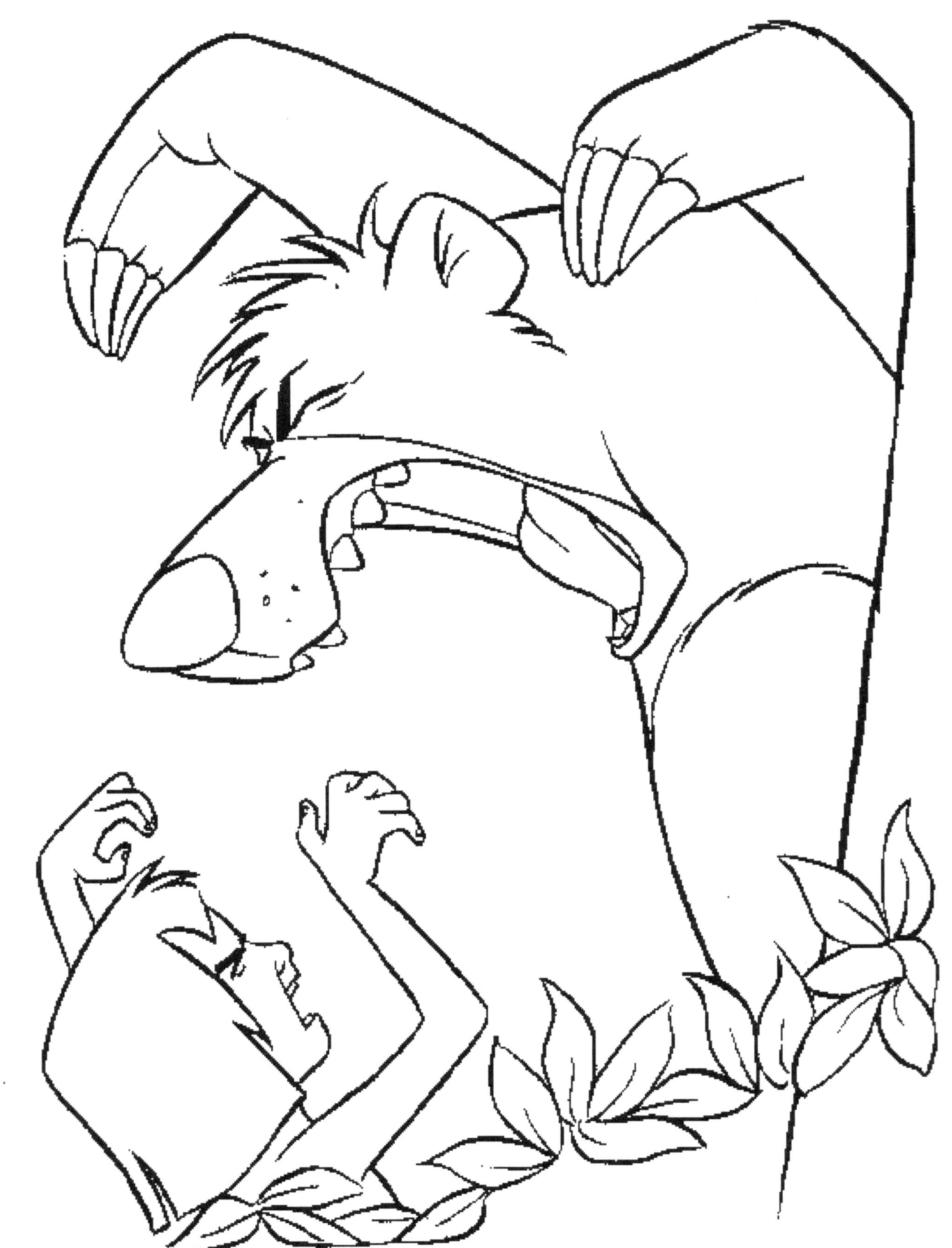

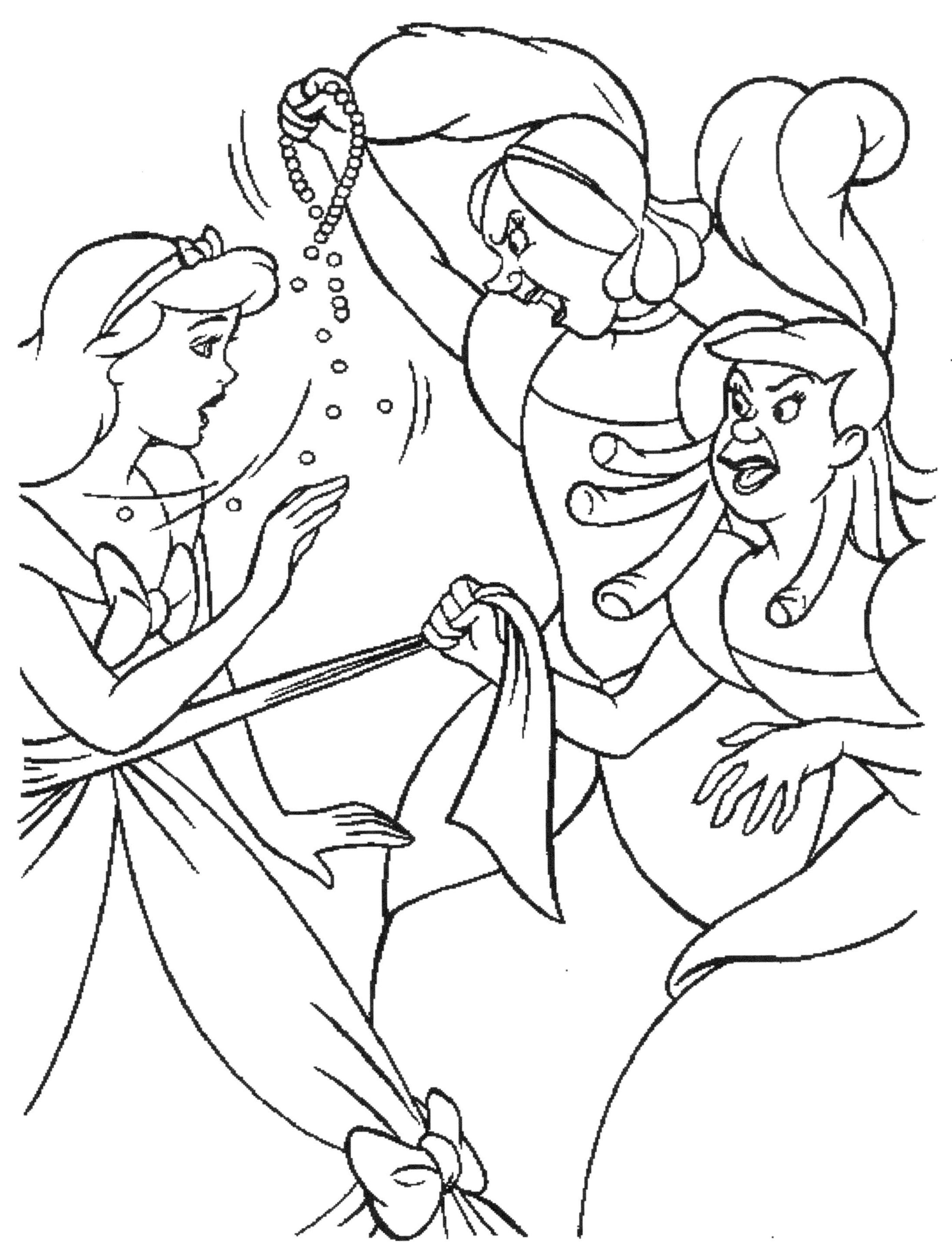

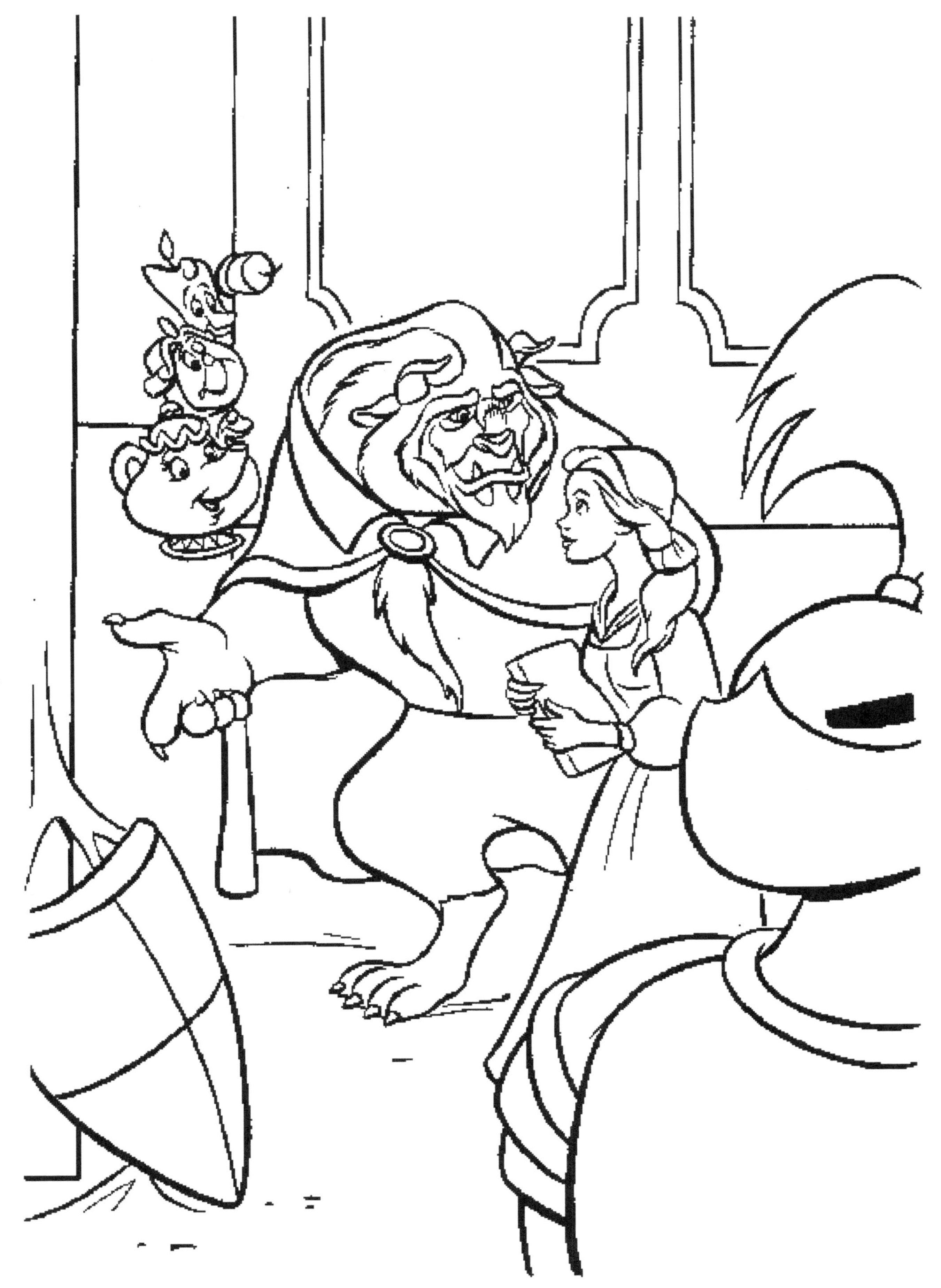

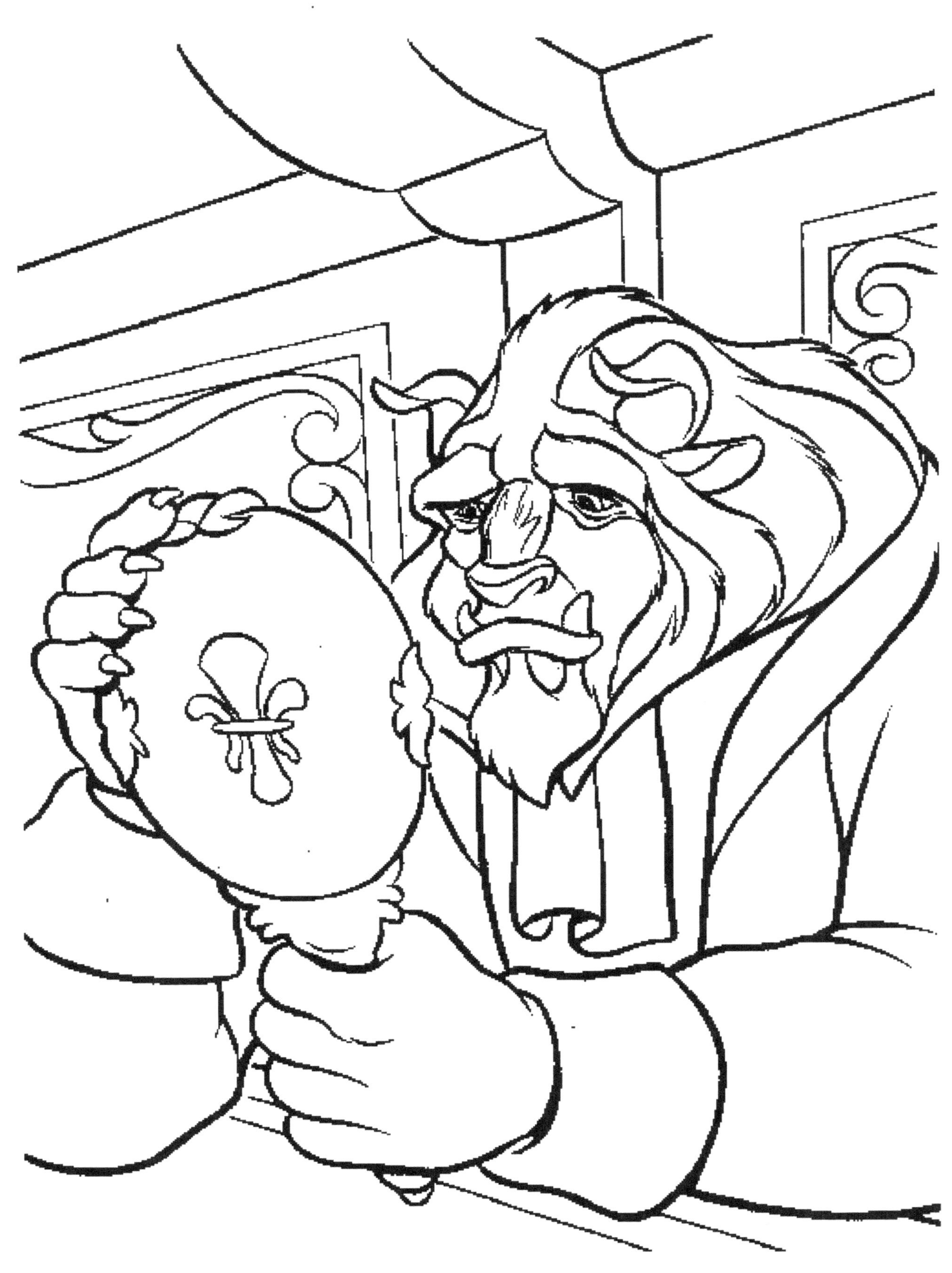

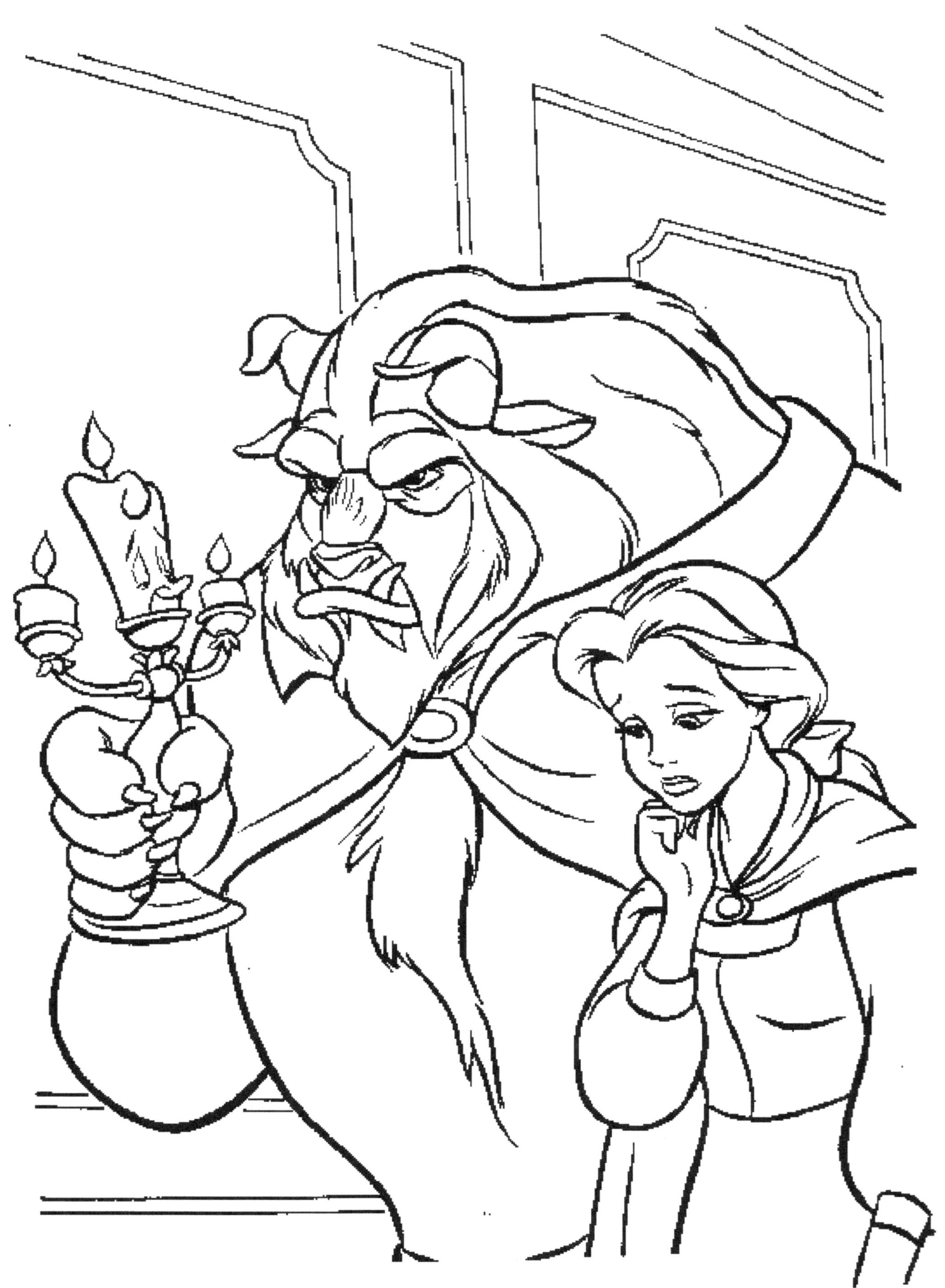

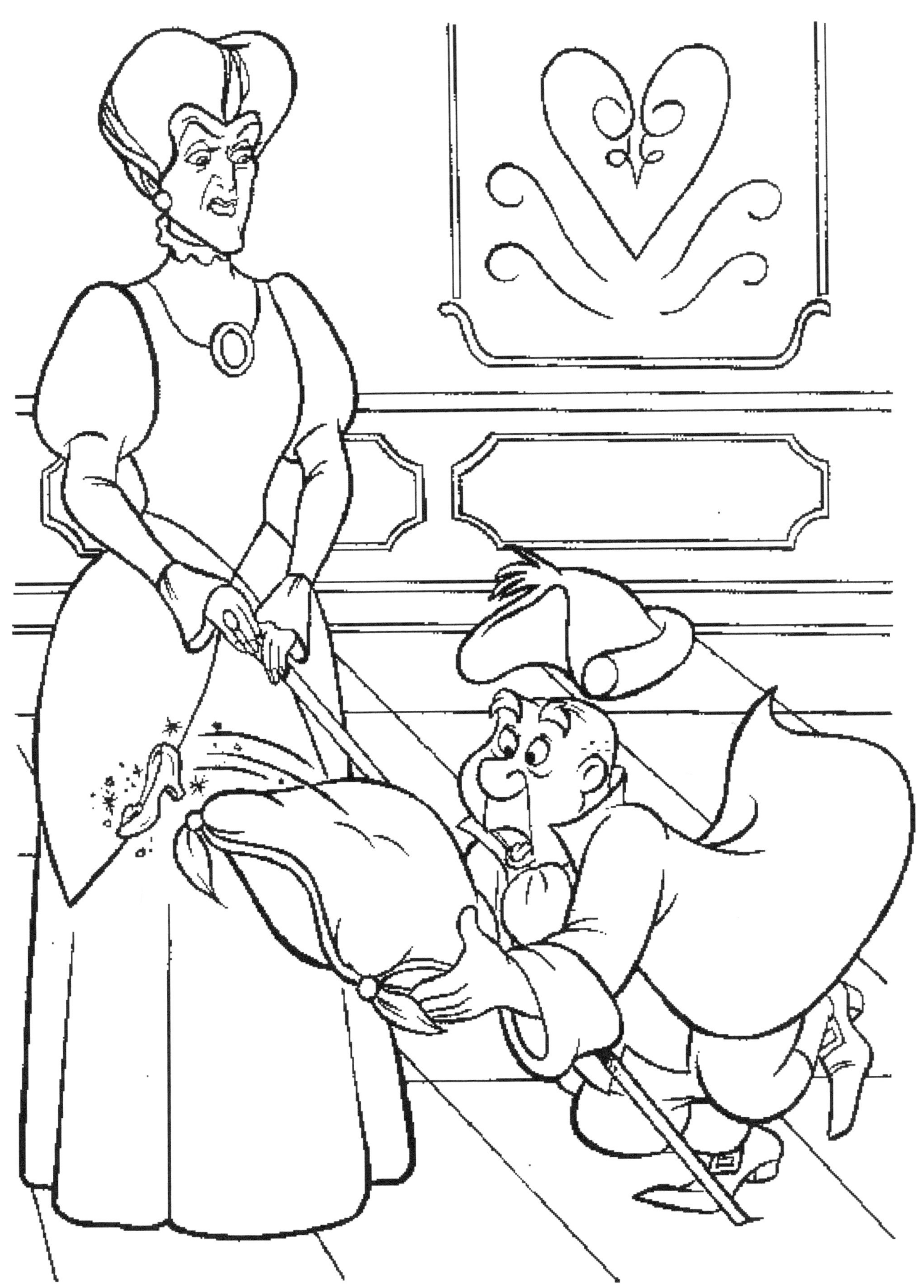

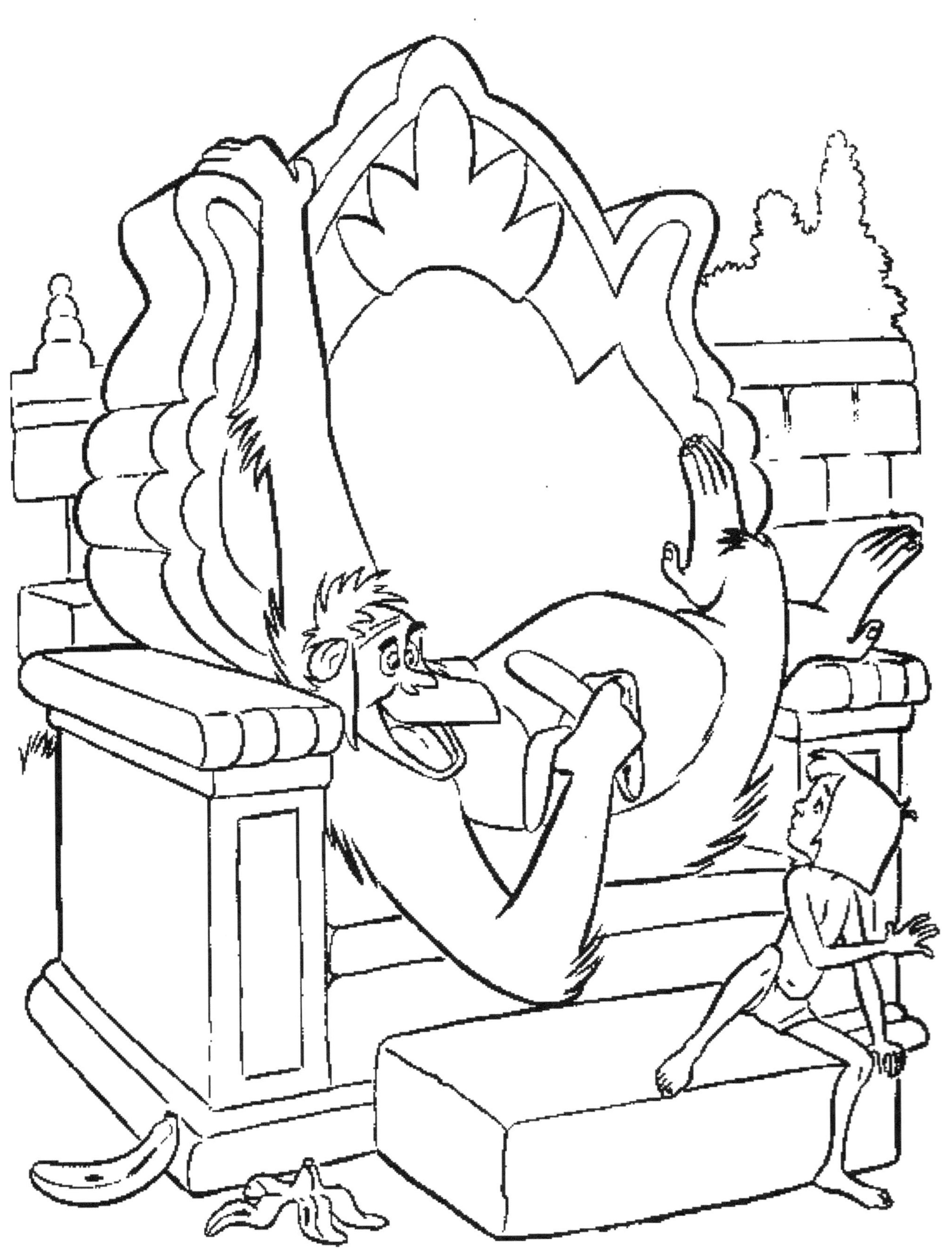

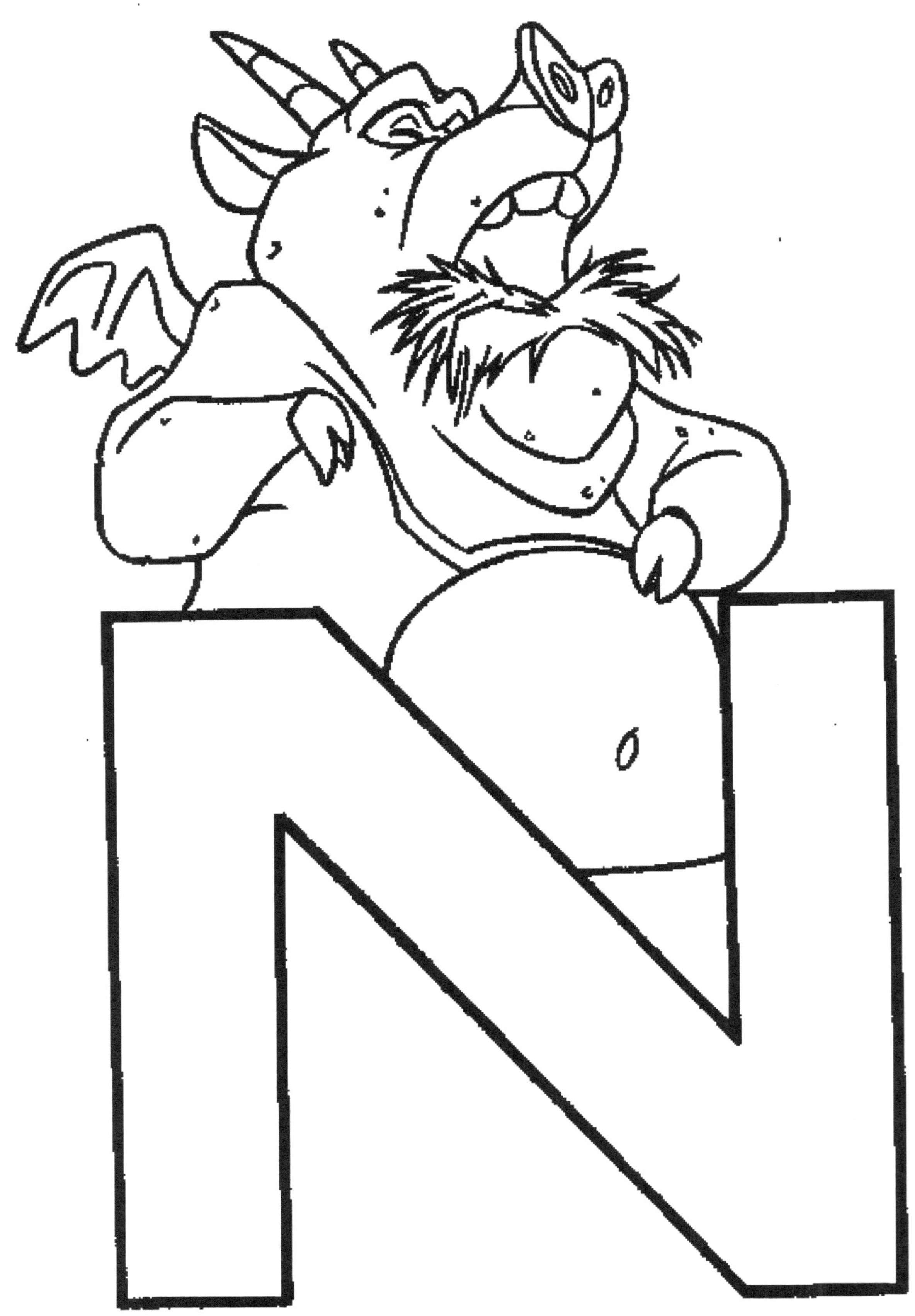

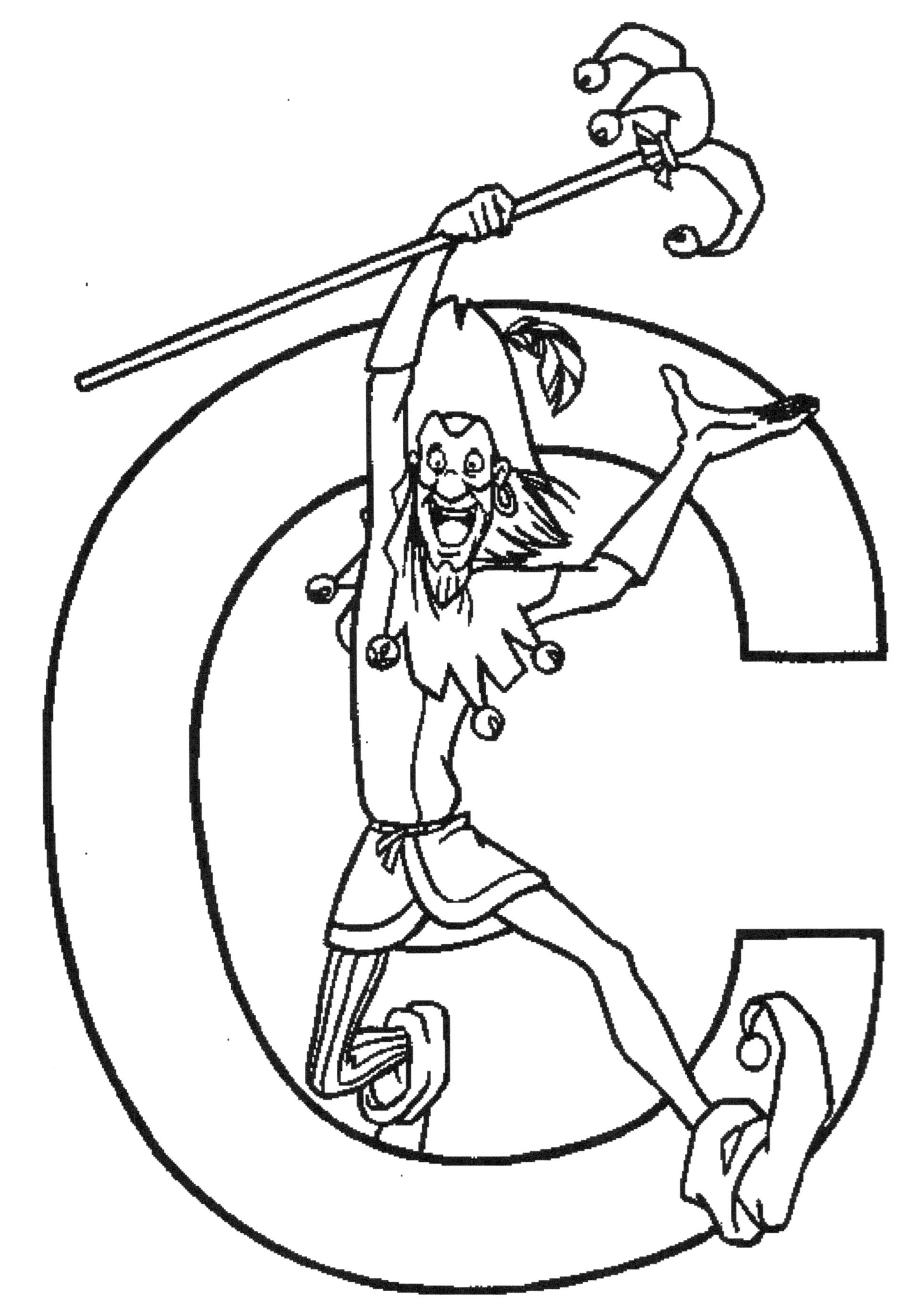

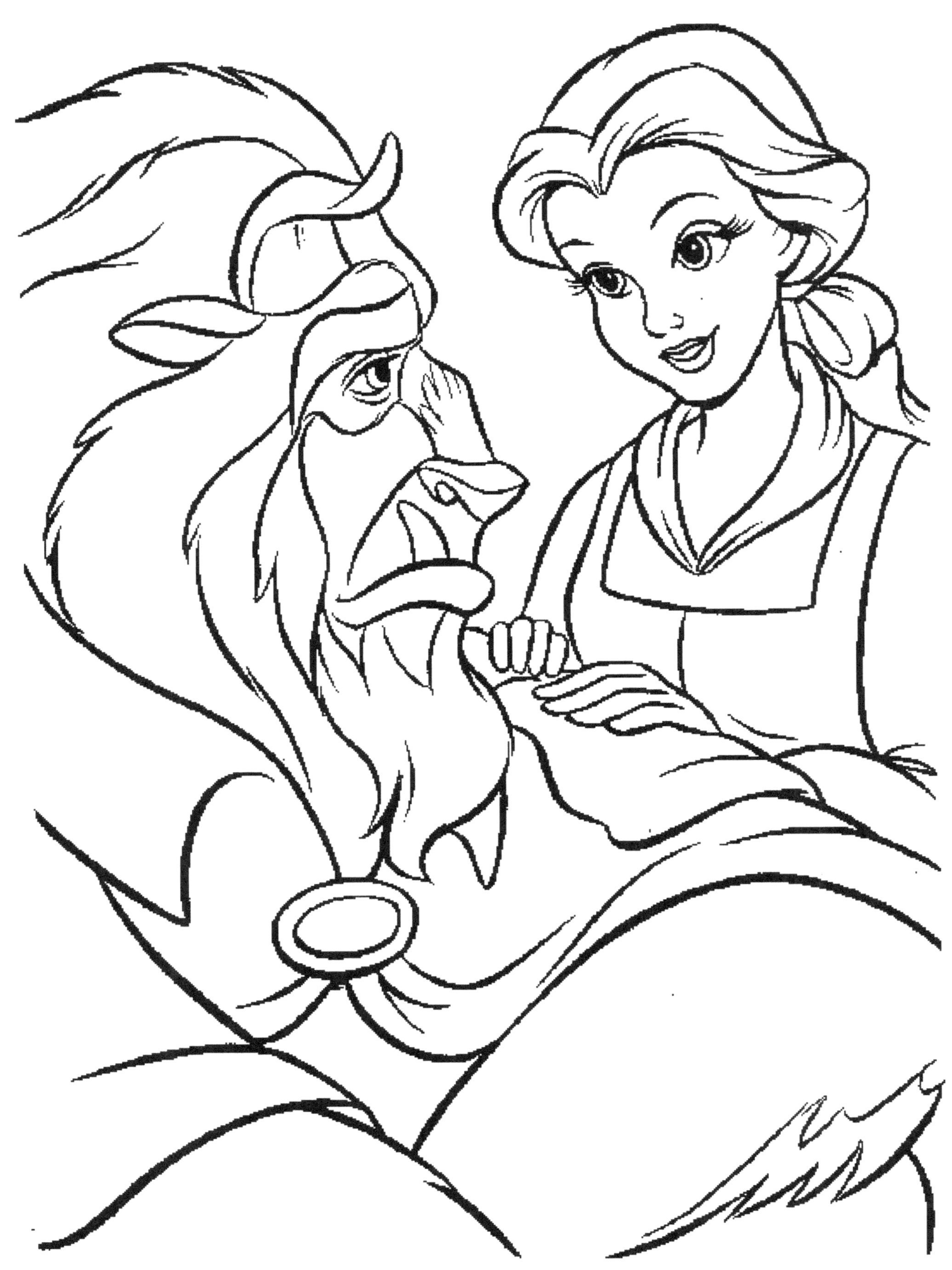

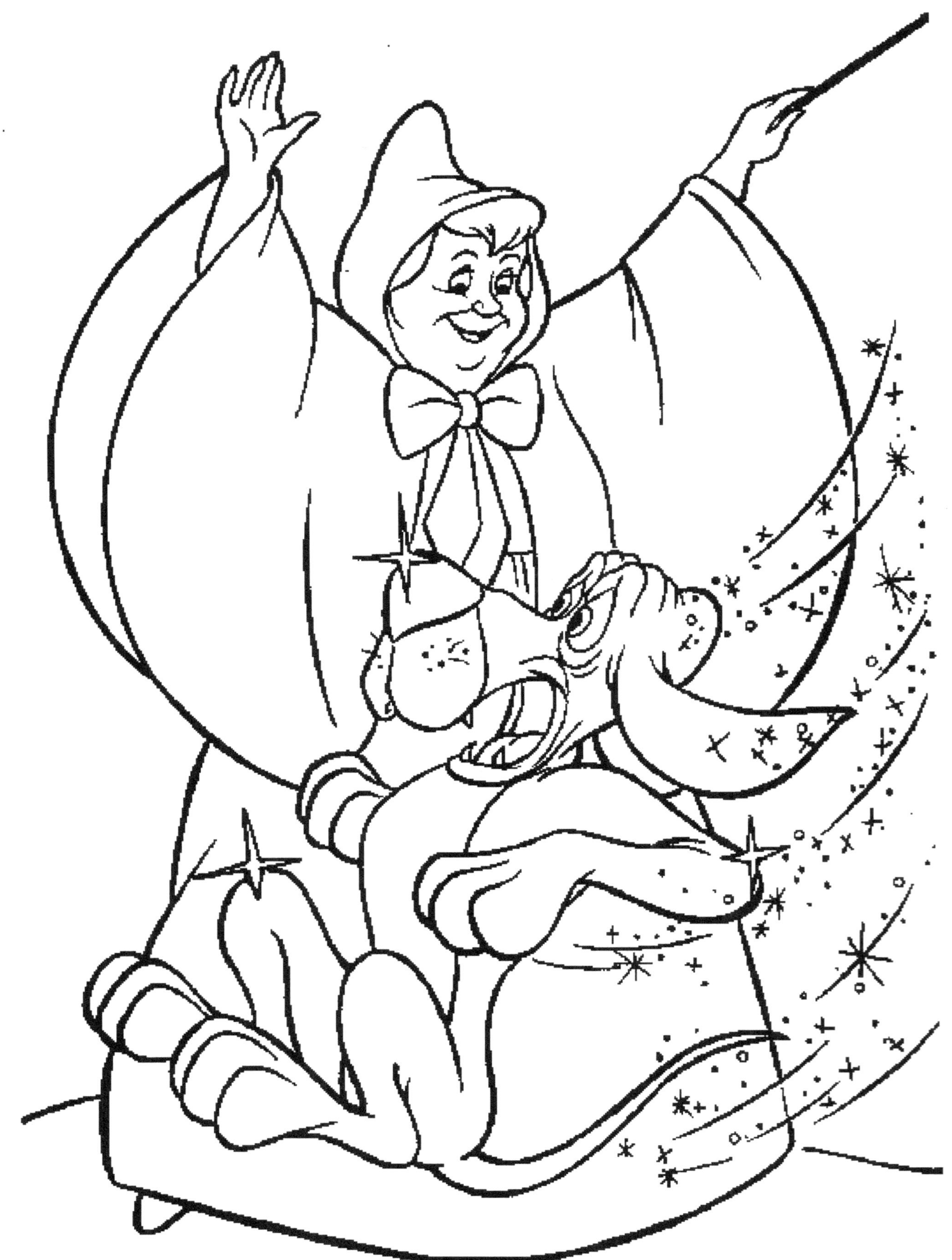

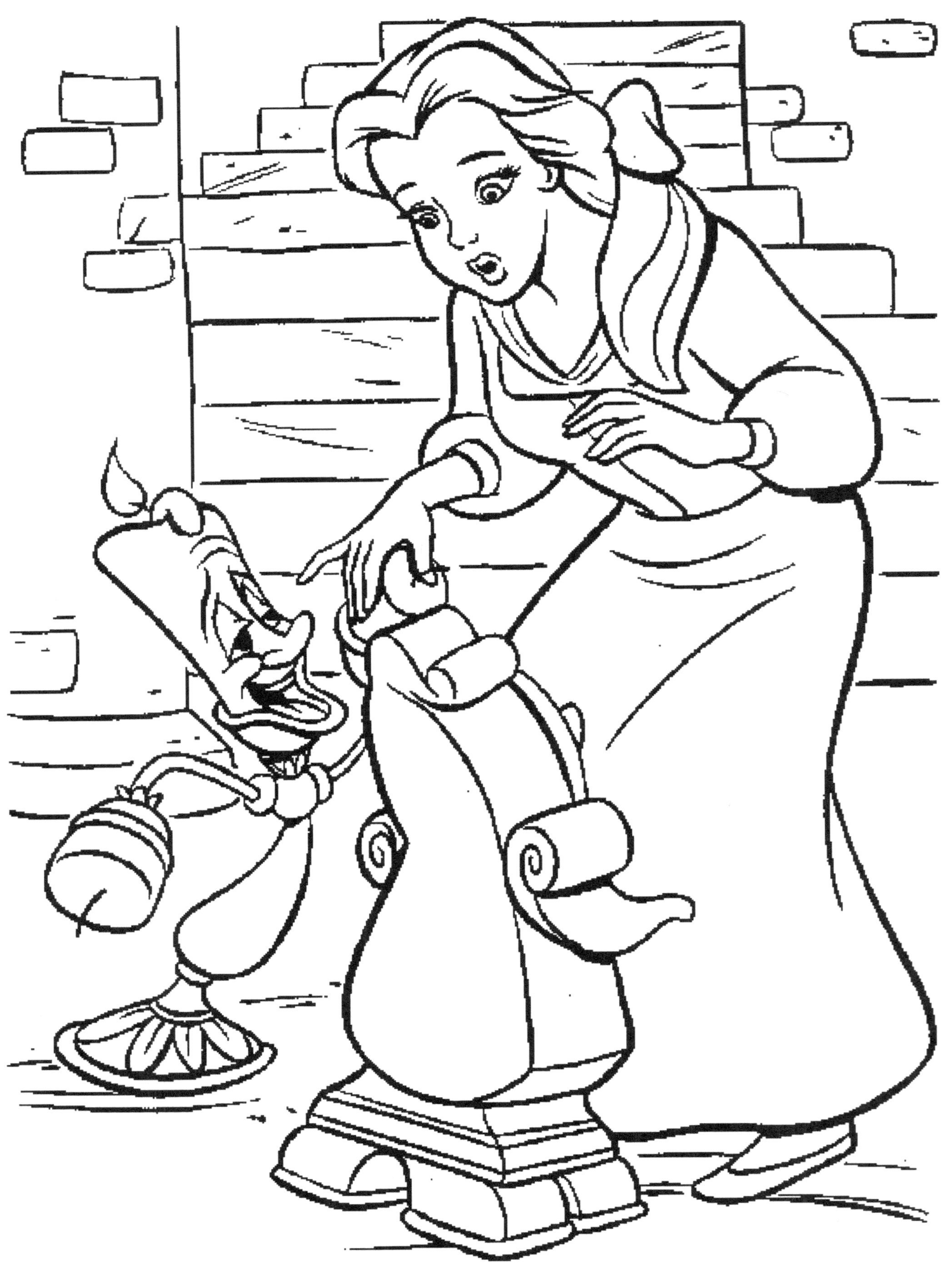

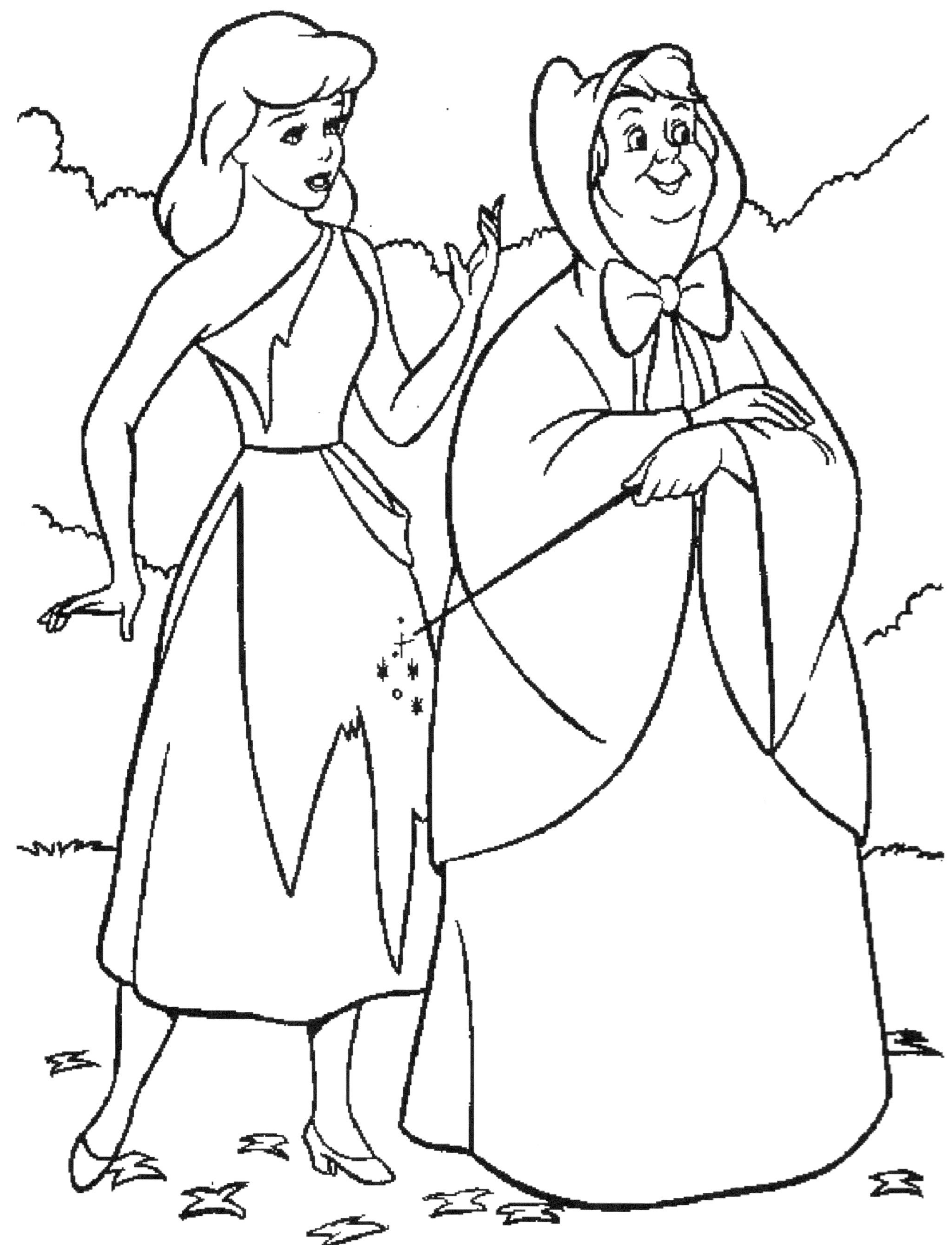

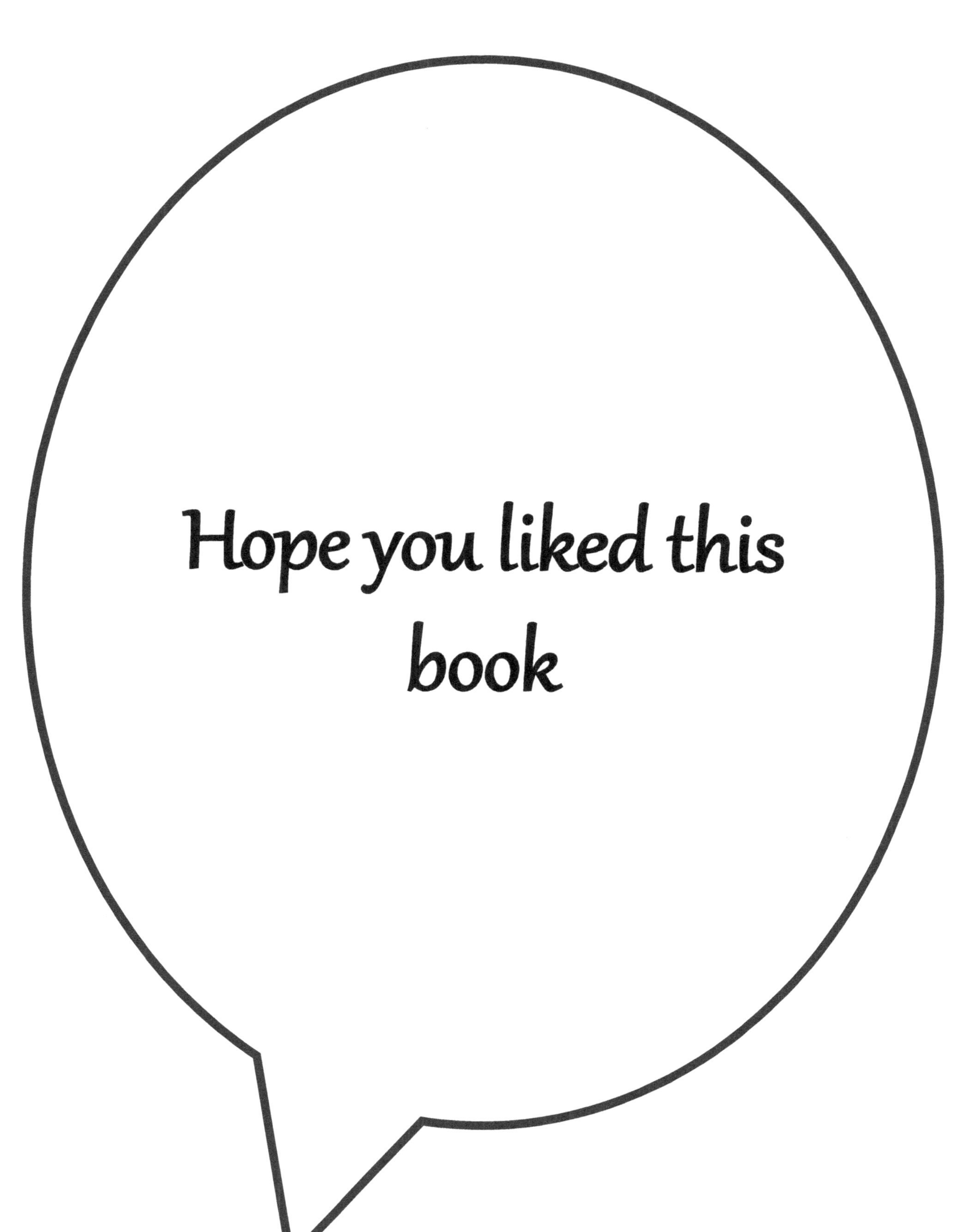
Hope you liked this book

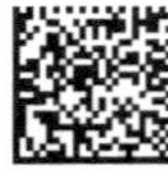